Succeeding Without Leading

Succeeding Without Leading:
How to Create a Successful Career in a Non-Leadership Role

Jennifer Raschig

Published by Raschig Creative Works
for Jennifer Raschig
Copyright 2019 Jennifer Raschig.

All rights reserved. No part of this publication may be reproduced, distributed or transmitted in any form or by any means including photocopying, recording, or other electronic or mechanical methods, without the prior written permission of the publisher, except in the case of brief quotations embodied in critical reviews and certain other noncommercial uses permitted by copyright law. For permission requests, contact the publisher at the address listed.

Print Edition ISBN: 9781086782356

First Printing: 2019

Raschig Creative Works
W2190 Turner Rd
Jefferson, WI 53549

Acknowledgements

This book would not have been possible without the guidance of the mentors in my life. Maureen and Carrie - thank you from the bottom of my heart. To my editors and beta readers, I appreciate your advice and criticisms. You have inspired me to think more deeply about this project and make changes I wouldn't have thought of. Thanks to you, this book is much better than it would have been otherwise.

Table of Contents

Introduction 1
Part 1: Defining Followers and Leaders 3
    Chapter 1 - Leadership isn't for everyone 5
    Chapter 2 - What being a follower is NOT 9
    Chapter 3 - Rewards of being a follower 10
Part 2: Successful Followers 13
    Chapter 4 - Defining success 15
    Chapter 5 - Traits of successful followers 19
    Chapter 6 - Learn more about yourself to find your
        best fit 29
Part 3: Your Organization, Your Leader, and You 45
    Chapter 7 - Identify a good organization and leader/
        follower fit 47
    Chapter 8 - Communication with your leader 55
    Chapter 9 - Flex to match your leader's style 65
Part 4: What's Next 73
    Chapter 10 - Moving in, out, here and there 75
    Chapter 11 - Asked to lead 80
    Chapter 12 - Still want to lead 85
    Chapter 13 - Final thoughts 89
Appendix 91
Resources 93
About the Author 97

Introduction

Despite the career moves you've made, you feel like there's something missing. Everything you read about career success and job satisfaction seems to point you to moving into a leadership position. You feel like a failure because you are never going to get that opportunity. Or, if you've achieved some level of people leadership, maybe you've discovered you're not fulfilled in that role. Or worse, maybe you feel like you're not doing a great job leading or managing the people reporting to you. What's wrong with you?!?

As it turns out - nothing. Have you stopped to question if being in a leadership role is the right path for you? Maybe you don't think you can have fulfillment in your job if you're not constantly moving up the proverbial ladder. Maybe you wonder if you can have a successful career outside of leadership. Of course you can!

In the following pages, you'll discover why not everyone is cut out to be a leader. You could be one of those people (and you'll learn that this is NOT a failure or personality flaw). You'll learn how to define your own personal success. This is different for everyone. You'll be able to identify or maybe even create the best job suited for your version of success. Doesn't that sound better than trying to fit into a position that doesn't suit your strengths or personality?

Along with identifying the right kind of job, you'll discover how you can recognize the type of leader that you would work well with. You will also pick up techniques to use when you're working for someone else who isn't a great leader - or who isn't the ideal leader for you.

As with many things worth doing, uncovering your version of success can be difficult. It takes work, self-reflection and, sometimes, daring. Nevertheless, it is absolutely achievable. The goal of this book is not to kill your dreams of being a leader of people - although you might find yourself creating a new dream. The goal is to help you discover if your path to success is in an area outside of people leadership – to guide you in finding that version of success, and to take pride in what you've chosen as your path. Are you ready to find your success?

Part 1: Defining Followers and Leaders

Jennifer Raschig

Chapter 1 - Leadership Isn't For Everyone

Have you ever witnessed a super-star employee be promoted through the ranks to management, only to watch them crash and burn as they try to lead people? This happened to Jose, a super-star software engineer. Upper management has had their eyes on him for quite a while. When a new supervisor position came open, Jose's boss immediately pegged him for the job. Jose has worked on some really tough assignments and he's the go-to guy when something is needed. So, he was promoted. . . and was immediately overwhelmed. He was tired all the time and he missed doing the hands-on coding work. The team he was leading wasn't nearly as productive as Jose's manager expected it to be. Unfortunately, Jose didn't have the time to step in and do the work that he might have done as an engineer. He was too busy dealing with "people" issues, something he had never done before and didn't find any joy in. Now he feels like a failure, when before, his job success buoyed him every day.

Can you relate to Jose? You may have heard of the "Peter Principle." Laurence Peter, an educator, theorized that people are promoted based on the work they are currently doing, not necessarily on their ability to do the work required in the new position. Essentially, people are promoted until they are incompetent. These employees may not be incompetent in every aspect of their position, but they are ineffectual in enough areas that they are not performing well. Let's face it, not everyone is cut out to lead people, despite what all the self-help books tell you. Leadership isn't a talent that everyone is born with. While some aspects of leadership can be learned, not everyone will be able to master the skills needed to be a great (or even good) leader.

It's important to understand this. You might feel like a failure if you aren't moving into management positions, or maybe you are the super-star who bombed in the leader role. But if you can come to appreciate that success is not defined by being a manager or director (or whatever other title you want to put to leadership positions), you'll be able to find fulfillment in following a different path for your career. Wouldn't you rather be successful in a job that you have the right skill set for? Or would you prefer constantly struggling with being in over your head just because you're clinging to a definition of success that isn't right for you? Sounds like an easy choice.

What exactly is a leader? It seems like it would be obvious, right? The Merriam-Webster Online Dictionary defines a leader as "a person who has commanding authority or influence." Although there are multiple areas of your life that you could technically lead in, let's focus on the workplace. When I refer to a leader, I'm specifically talking about a person in an organization or business that oversees the work of others - those who have 'commanding authority.'

Certainly, individuals can hold titles that connote leadership positions. Yet they are not overseeing other people's work. They might be directing a process or strategy. This is the "influence" part of leadership, as defined by Merriam-Webster. I am not speaking about that aspect of leadership. I think we all have the ability to influence others, in some capacity, in our jobs. This is a critical trait of a good follower, too. (By the way, I'll get into traits of great followers in later chapters.)

You might have heard something along the lines of "everyone is a leader." That's true... in part. Someone may do very well "leading" their home or serving in their church or community organization. Those roles are considered leadership - but don't require all the same skills needed to lead other adults in a job setting. The same person who is an incredible coach may not be cut out to be a leader in the workplace.

Even if it's your biggest desire to be a leader of people, you might have to face the fact that you just don't have the right skills to be truly successful, or even remotely satisfied in a position of leadership. I've experienced this happening with past employees who have reported to me.

In one case, I knew "George" did not have the personality or the ingrained character traits to be a truly great leader. He and I talked about what leadership entails. We discussed the traits and skills required to be successful in that capacity. Then, I helped him establish mentoring relationships with other managers. Shadowing opportunities were given - and still George wanted to go down the path of leadership. Less than 3 months after securing a position as a supervisor, he realized people leadership wasn't for him and began looking for a way out of that position.

Maybe you've watched the hit television show, *Shark Tank*, where entrepreneurs pitch their businesses to wealthy financiers (the "sharks"), hoping to get someone to invest in their company. At times, the shark will choose not to invest because the entrepreneur simply doesn't have the chops to run a business. The investor might say something like, "You're a terrific salesman, but I don't think you have what it takes to lead a business."

The potential backer recognizes that the person presenting their business just doesn't have the right skill set to achieve success in the leadership role of the company - and it's not worth losing their investment. And, just like the wealthy investor points out to the entrepreneur that she is a successful salesperson or inventor, you can be wildly successful in another area and not be a leader. Many examples are available to us showing when individuals recognized they weren't leaders, and when someone with the right skills took over from an unskilled leader making the organization more successful that it would have been.

John Riccardo was just one of those examples. In 1978, he was the chairman and chief executive of Chrysler Corporation. The company was going through some very rocky times and John knew he didn't have the right experience and skills to get the company through the challenges it was facing. John recruited Lee Iacocca to join the company because he realized Mr. Iacocca would be able to lead Chrysler away from destruction. Although near retirement, Riccardo was still successful. He took on a different role to campaign in Washington D.C. for financial assistance for the company. That campaigning eventually led to a government loan and survival for Chrysler.

Riccardo recognized his leadership had a lid. It takes quite a bit of self-reflection to understand your own limits. It also requires a good deal of humility - and possibly sacrifice. John Riccardo is in rare company. Most often, people don't recognize their limited leadership capacity, and unfortunately, their inability is proven when someone else takes over. That is exactly what happened to the McDonald brothers.

While Richard and Maurice McDonald had a great concept and made many innovations to jumpstart the fast food industry, McDonald's would not have grown into the world power it is today without the vision and leadership of Ray Kroc.

Years after the brothers started their hamburger stand, Kroc, a milkshake mixer salesman, came along with a much bigger vision for the company. Richard and Maurice were content to keep the company small and only franchise a few locations.

Kroc, now acting as their franchising agent, eventually persuaded the McDonalds to sell him the entire company, including the McDonald name. Obviously, he was quite successful in carrying out his vision. McDonald's Corporation is now (as of this writing) the largest restaurant business in the world. Kroc is seen as the founder of McDonald's, despite the company's launching decades earlier by Ray and Maurice.

It's interesting to compare the above examples. If you choose to take a role that is better suited to your skill set, you can have individual success and make a big impact - just as John Riccardo did. If you don't recognize the limits to your leadership abilities, like the McDonald brothers, you might fade into obscurity and not be recognized for your contributions.

Chapter 2 - What being a follower is NOT

For some reason there is a negative connotation when it comes to the word "follower." Perhaps because most people associate following with being sheep, following blindly along with no thought or decision-making of their own. I believe this is a misunderstanding of being a follower in the workplace. Even if you're not the leader, you don't have to follow blindly like a sheep.

Following doesn't mean that you need to disappear, either. I suppose if you really don't want to be recognized, and you want to fade into the background, you can do that. You don't have to, though. You should be recognized for your contributions and good work. A good leader will do this, so be prepared for the recognition.

A follower is not a wallflower. This book is about not being a wallflower. Successful followers find ways to stand out from their peers - to be recognized for their achievements. Being recognized, however, does not always mean moving up into a leadership position.

A follower is not someone who never has their ideas heard. You don't need to put your head down and keep quiet. In fact, when you contribute to an organization, you are more valuable to them. No matter what your job is, it's important that you fully engage in your role by participating in all aspects.

You don't have to let someone else, including your manager or boss, "walk" on you. If you're asked to do something you're uncomfortable with (because it's dangerous, unethical, etc.), speak up. Go to your boss and talk with them - having a solution or workaround in mind.

By the way, the best leaders have respect for those that follow them. They understand that without people working with them that know how to do their job well, they wouldn't be successful in their own jobs. As a successful follower, you will be able to find leaders who have this quality. You will give respect and receive it. You shouldn't tolerate anything less.

Chapter 3 - Rewards of Being a Follower

You may be asking yourself why should you be a follower instead of a leader? What's in it for you? Especially when everyone else seems to think you need to be moving up to be going somewhere. You might get the impression they think you're going nowhere. Well, that's flawed reasoning. There are more directions than up.

The view from the top (or even near the top) isn't always great. While each job you have has some level of responsibility, the higher up the corporate ladder you go, the more accountability you have. To borrow a phrase from Harry Truman, the buck stops here. The leader is always responsible. Management positions can be more stressful - much of the stress due to the increased responsibility. So, next time you're getting a bit jealous of being passed over for a promotion, remember the stress and responsibility that comes along with that.

An executive leader I once worked with confided that he hadn't really wanted to be promoted to the role he was in. He had previously switched companies so that he could step away from the vice president position he had been promoted to. The time commitment and stress involved weren't worth the pay. He was seriously considering leaving his current company (where he is viewed as "successful") because of the stress associated with that level of leadership.

While some stress is good (as you'll find in the next chapter), we have to gauge when it's affecting us physically and emotionally. Too much stress can have a negative effect.

You also need to consider the relationships you can have on the job. Work friendships are very important to job satisfaction according to a 2017 Gallup report on workplaces in America. But those in a leadership role don't have the same opportunities to form those workplace friendships. They must maintain a professional distance and strong boundaries. You, as a follower, can seek out friendships across your organization, without too much fear of the appearance of the relationship.

As a follower, you are also more likely to feel like part of a team. Consider the number of peers you have and how that would decrease as you move to higher roles. You have fewer people to share the workload with.

Most importantly, you'll likely be happier. I'm not saying that correctly placed leaders aren't happy. However, I am saying if you force yourself into a job that you aren't prepared or suited for, you won't be happy. You'll get more enjoyment out of spreading your wings in a position that you're more suited for. From happiness springs success.

This may be different from what you imagined. The prevailing thought has been that to be happy you must first be successful, then happiness will follow. That's simply not true - and has been disproved through research. In his book, *The Happiness Advantage,* author and Harvard lecturer Shawn Achor asserts that if we wait to be "happy" until after we're successful, we're limiting our potential to be successful. We can't depend on our success to make us happy. Our brain will use our positive attitude - our happiness - to drive performance through increased creativity, productivity and motivation. Thus, you find success through happiness driving your performance.

Once you get past the erroneous thought that to be in charge is to succeed, you'll discover many benefits of remaining a follower. As you continue working for others, you'll find different rewards in the form of organizational success. You're doing your best work for a leader that believes in you. Your team will be successful because of your contributions. You'll be valued and appreciated.

If you truly are destined for leadership, being a great follower will only set you up for that climb up the ladder. The roles aren't mutually exclusive. While I maintain that not everyone can or should be a leader, you may very well be reading this book and be headed for a leader position. If you have other leadership skills and you've learned to be a great follower, it is possible to move into a role managing the work of others. You can and will, because your voice will be heard, you will be contributing, and you will garner the respect of others.

Jennifer Raschig

Part 2: Successful Followers

Jennifer Raschig

Chapter 4 - Defining Success

I've established that success shouldn't necessarily be defined only as gaining a position of people leadership with a fancy title. Then what is success? How do you know when you've achieved it? Success isn't a one-size-fits-all concept. You're not the same as that annoying co-worker that's always bragging about his association with the big-wigs, right? He might feel very successful in his position because of his opportunities to rub elbows with "important" people. Your achievement is different because you're different. Accomplishment can be defined in a number of ways. This leads to being able to realize success through multiple avenues. You should, however, work to define your personal success so you can create goals around attaining it.

Increase in Income

Some might define success as an increase in salary or income. An increase in pay absolutely can come without being promoted into leadership. I completely understand that having a specific standard of income could, at least initially, be your definition of achievement. You should consider thoughtfully what that level is. I would caution, however, that money should not be your only definition of success. The pursuit of money above all else typically will not lead to a feeling of accomplishment. I experienced this in my own life when I realized that I didn't feel successful, even when I hit my goal of a six-figure income. I felt there was more for me to achieve and I had to re-evaluate my goals and definition of success. It's important to understand that to get to a higher income, you might need to make choices about your career that otherwise don't fit with your lifestyle. Weigh the pros and cons of an opportunity for an increased salary in a new position very carefully. Life holds so much more than a high income.

Increase in Knowledge

Attaining success could be described by some as an increase in knowledge. Learning is a critical component of success in the workplace. If you're not learning, you'll remain stagnant. You won't be able to adapt to changes in technology and information. The same old way of doing things will no longer work. So, it's important to be a lifelong learner. For most people, however, simply obtaining knowledge is not a definition of success. Are you looking for knowledge in a specific area? How do you apply that knowledge? How do you know when you've reached your goal of "obtaining knowledge?"

Increase in Flexibility

Maybe success to you is being in a job where you are able to choose the hours you work. That's true for many people. You could consider if your current position, or future opportunities, will give you the flexibility to achieve the work/life balance you are looking for. It could be that nothing else matters as long as you have that.

Increase in Prestige

For others, prestige could be the factor that signifies their idea of success. You may wonder how you can obtain recognition without becoming a leader. Prestige is not all about having an important job title. Prestige is admiration based on the perception of your achievements. So, think of your reputation as your job title. Your reputation advertises who you are, much more specifically than a fancy title would. Success, defined as "prestige," would mean having an outstanding reputation at your organization, and even beyond your current company. If you have opportunity to interact with other companies through your role, or maybe even community organizations, your reputation will reach far and wide.

The True Definition

With all these possibilities of how you might define success, how do you know when you're successful? How do you figure out that you've landed in the job and role that you're meant for? It helps to know what motivates you, so that you can ultimately express your achievement based on your values. Rick Whitted, in his best-seller *Outgrow Your Space at Work: How to thrive at work and build a successful career*, walks you through how you can figure out what your values are and the emotional motivators you have for career growth. Understanding what you value and what your motivators are and how they align is important because it will help you make clear career choices that align with who you are and what your specific goals are.

Once you consider the different aspects that go into success and determine what your values and emotional motivators are, you might come to the realization that success is about satisfaction. Being at a place in your career where you're still learning, you're being paid appropriately for your expertise and experience, your life is balanced as you want it to be, and you are being recognized for what you contribute. That is true success.

Now, there might be elements of this definition of success that are more important to you than others. Maybe you feel like real success is being recognized and that trumps learning or earning a raise. That's okay. Individual satisfaction is unique. Success contains multiple components.

The Value of Growth

What happens when you achieve what you perceive as success - do you hang out in your job because you've reached the pinnacle? That depends. Are you still satisfied with your position? Is it still meeting your needs to learn? If you're still passionate about what you do, there is no reason to feel pressured to move on!

There seems to be a stigma in society of being content with where you are, but there shouldn't be. It's important to look internally to see if there is a need for change, rather than being prompted to consider something else just because you've been in your position for a certain amount of time. But, when you get to the point that you are no longer growing or feel like your position isn't something you're passionate about, success has moved for you.

Growth is important to your success. And to grow, you have to be under a certain amount of stress. Think about how humans grow physically. The muscle has to be stressed to grow larger - to gain. Stressing allows new connections to form and more muscle to build. This applies to growth in other areas, including your career.

Just like with muscle stress, you don't want it to be painful. That's the bad kind of stress we talked about in the last chapter. Good stress stretches us just enough to grow. Challenge yourself to be under stress to be successful. Once you achieve the goal, challenge yourself to new goals. You are successful because you achieved what you set out to do, but to continue in your success, you need to set new goals that are challenging to provide growth.

Let's build on the idea of defining your personal success. If each individual has a unique perspective on what success on the job means - keeping in mind that it ultimately leads to satisfaction - then you need to define your goals that, when met, signify your success.

Do you currently have career goals? What are they based on? If your goals are based on moving up the corporate ladder just because you "should," rethink your goals!

Chapter 5 - Traits of Successful Followers

Everyone is a follower. What makes the difference between followers who are not satisfied in their jobs and successful followers who are satisfied? Is it that the less satisfied followers are not growing or learning? Just as leaders have important qualities that make them stand out and lead successfully, followers also have specific traits that enable them to find success.

Thriving followers understand how to frame their goals, how to build relationships and how to identify their unique strengths and talents. They also possess specific characteristics that give them a boost to achieving their success. They are determined and take initiative. Great followers also tend to be morale boosters and servants. Let's explore each of these.

Understand their own goals

At the end of the previous chapter, I mentioned goals briefly, challenging you to rethink your goals if they are based on moving up the corporate ladder. If you had the chance to design your life, what would it look like? Would you be in a position that you could work remotely from anywhere? Or, would you want to be in a role that you were surrounded by like-minded team members. Maybe you would be doing something completely different than what you are doing today. Take time to dream about where you really want to be and then set your goals around these ideas.

When you take the time to re-examine your goals, you must be sure you are setting the right kind of goals. You may have heard the term SMART goals before (usually in the context of a performance review or goal setting session at work). You can use this concept for your career and life goals in general. SMART is an acronym that stands for specific, measurable, attainable, relevant and time-based. Successful people set SMART goals.

It's important that you understand each of these elements and that any goal you create for yourself contains all the components for a SMART goal. You can use the "W" questions (who, what, why, when) to help you. The first element, "specific," seems to be self-explanatory. For the sake of clarity, let's define it. A specific goal is one that is focused and well-defined. Stop thinking in broad terms. Home in on what you really want and make that your goal. You use several of the "W" questions in creating a specific goal. Knowing 'why' you are setting this goal will help you define what is needed to move forward – whether it's fixing a problem or achieving something new. You will also use the 'who' and 'what' questions here. Who will be needed to act on this goal? Is it just you, or do you require the participation of others? Be sure to identify that in your goal. Of course, the 'what' gets at the meat of the matter. What is it that needs to be accomplished?

Then, think about how you are going to make your goal measurable. All this means is there needs to be some way to determine that you're making progress toward your goal. At some point, you'll need a way to measure that you've achieved it.

Next, consider if the goal is attainable. Do you currently possess the skills necessary to achieve the goal? If not, include in your goal how you will obtain those skills.

Depending on the type of goal you're setting, relevancy can mean different things – and may not matter in the end. Go back to 'why' you are setting the goal. You may want to learn how to bake fantastic pastries, but unless that has something to do with your career, it's not relevant.

The last element is time-based. This is the 'when.' By what point should this goal be accomplished? The time element may be dependent on other aspects – such as obtaining different skills or reaching other milestones. For example, someone might create their goal to be working remotely in a (specific) position for a (specific) company by the time their oldest child graduates college. Or, maybe, the goal is to be completed six months after obtaining a license or degree in a new field.

It's not difficult to set SMART goals, but it takes practice. Setting good goals also requires significant thought. You have to keep digging to figure out what goal you'll set that will answer your "why" question. To help you in setting SMART goals, I've included a worksheet in the Appendix that you can use to be sure you're answering each component of the goal. Using a worksheet or template can also ensure that you write your goals down – which is vitally important to your success in attaining them. A study by Gail Matthews, PHD, a psychology professor at Dominican University of California, provides empirical evidence that people who write their goals achieve significantly more of them than those who only think about their goals. What's more, creating actionable steps and being accountable to report on your progress to a friend allows even greater achievements. If you can, find an accountability partner to help you stay on track.

Okay, now is the time to think about your goals. Put the book down and establish those goals before you move on.

Identify their strengths and talents

Chapter 6 goes in depth into identifying strengths and talents, so this will just be an overview here. You may have taken different personality or skills tests in the past. Those are very good places to start. Keep in mind that you may need to reach out to others in your circle of influence (family, friends, coworkers) to get a complete picture of your unique mix of strengths. Unfortunately, humans are somewhat biased – whether positively or negatively – when reflecting on our own talents. You must be comfortable reaching out to others to get feedback on their perceptions and interactions with you. When you've polled those who know you well, combine their feedback with your own reflections to get a realistic picture of where you shine. Then, you can use that knowledge in creating your success.

Possess specific characteristics

While you may not naturally exhibit all the character traits in this section, you can always focus on those qualities to improve your use of them. You do have the ability to change the way you behave. Insight and commitment are necessary to push against your inherent tendencies. Growth in any area generally isn't easy. The effort will be rewarded multiple times over. As you focus on the following traits and contemplate how you use them, realize that lacking strength in any single trait doesn't mean you can't enjoy success as a follower. You'll need to rely on your other traits more. Resolve to do the work that will make the use of these qualities inherent to your very being and you will enjoy success.

What attributes should you focus on? One is determination. The Merriam-Webster dictionary defines determination as "a firm or fixed intention to achieve a desired end." With determination, you have the mindset to persevere when doors aren't opening for you, or your career isn't moving as fast as you think it should. Determination keeps you motivated when you are told no, or when you suffer failure in your career. It keeps you going when you don't feel like anyone is on your side.

If you've found yourself lacking determination (or willpower), you need strategies to improve. Building up determination largely involves mental exercises. Once you have made the decision to be determined, take the time to imagine yourself living with resolution. It may sound hokey to you. I get it – but psychologically, envisioning yourself being determined does increase your willpower overall. Think about a professional athlete that has a goal of winning a title or championship. In their quest to reach that level of success, they are told to imagine themselves being the champion. The vision provides motivation to keep moving forward. You can use the same technique. See yourself moving forward despite setbacks.

It's also helpful to control your stress level when it gets to the "painful" level. Stress is a demotivator. If you're feeling stressed, you often have negative thoughts and emotions which impact your willpower. Learn techniques to combat stress – get enough rest, exercise, and nutrition. We are total beings and our physical selves impact our emotional selves.

You can also practice using systems of rewards. Keeping up willpower, especially if it doesn't come naturally, zaps your strength. After staying focused and battling through setbacks, reward yourself. Rewards provide motivation to continue and provide breaks for your mental well-being.

Along with determination, you must have initiative. Followers who don't stand out wait for someone to tell them what to do. Successful followers act - they make things happen, without waiting for direction. How can you follow without direction? Well, that's a good question. You know what needs to be accomplished in your role and in your company. This requires being invested in what's going on around you and wanting to see success for the organization you work for. Then, you can assess what may need to be done, decide if you might have the skills to do it and go for it.

You might be thinking that you don't have that kind of leeway in your position. You're only allowed to do what you're told and that's it. The fact is, most people have about 80% of their positions "prescribed" and out of their control. According to *The Five Patterns of Extraordinary Careers: The guide for achieving success and satisfaction* by James Citrin and Richard Smith, workers can exercise at least some freedom in what they do the other 20% of the time. Use that 20% to increase your value to the company.

Increasing your value lets you stand out. Think about areas within the company that aren't doing as well, or perhaps an area that you believe you could help transform. Maybe you have some ideas that you believe could contribute to the company's success. Have a discussion with your boss about undertaking a special project that can help the organization move forward. Be open to doing something in exchange for the approval to go outside your boundaries. The willingness to take on something that is difficult, or maybe "grunt work" shows that you are truly committed to the company.

Taking on projects outside of your typical job description accomplishes a couple of things. First, as mentioned, it will increase your value and recognition in the company you work for. Secondly, it will give you additional experience with skills that you can use in other positions as you expand in your career.

That's all well and good for those of us who have that little bit of choice. But, I'm sure some of you are thinking, "I don't have that freedom to choose any part of my job!" The best thing to do in this situation is to change your perspective about different aspects of your work.

Instead of looking at it as a task you don't enjoy or that you can't make an impact with, refocus your thinking. How can you choose to look at it that will speak to your strengths or passions? Do you even know what your passions are? What energizes you at work?

Think about particular times that you felt you were operating at your best. What task were you doing and how did that relate to a broader vision. So, for example, if you were troubleshooting a technical problem, think about all the times you were trying to figure out what was wrong and fixing the issue. Were those energizing moments?

Can you connect that problem-solving strength to a task that you don't feel as successful in? Take paperwork, for example. If you must do paperwork associated with resolving an issue and you don't feel like you can shine in that - change your perspective. You are providing the solution to someone who might have the same issue. They can review your paperwork and fix the problem. While you might think you would become extraneous at that point, you are really becoming more successful by impacting more people. You are, in fact, solving another problem! At the same time, you are taking initiative to view your prescribed job tasks as something more. You will shine because your attitude has changed.

Successful followers also know how to boost coworkers' morale. Stick with me a minute on this one. I know it seems like you're helping their success and not your own. But employees who are looked upon as accomplished often encourage others in the workplace. They are in high demand because other employees want to work with them. Morale boosters are a big asset to any team.

If focusing on others' enjoyment doesn't come naturally to you, focus on doing some small things. Be kind! Say please and thank you. Be the person who appreciates the time and effort others put into their work. Along with that, strive to give credit where credit is due. Make it a habit to recognize your coworkers in meetings when they've contributed to a project or were helpful to you. You could also keep track of special dates (birthdays, anniversaries, etc.) to celebrate with them. You don't need to make it a public or group celebration, unless you want to, and it's allowed in your organization. Just quietly and consistently letting your coworkers know you are thinking about them (even if you have to have a calendar reminder to do it) will help boost their morale. Your efforts will be recognized in goodwill and recommendations from your coworkers.

Finally, successful followers will possess a servant attitude. No, this doesn't mean you need to wait on people and do their every bidding. But, approach your work with the thought that your role is to help others (your company, your boss, your coworkers) succeed. Gandhi once said, "The best way to find yourself is to lose yourself in the service of others." From the mouth of a great leader, we are counselled that serving others is important for our own growth.

Becoming a servant requires humility and patience. It also requires having a desire to help others succeed. If you need help in developing that desire (trust me, it doesn't always come naturally), remember that the more you give to other people, the more you will get in return. But, don't do something with the *expectation* that you'll get something out of it. I know that sounds contradictory. Think of it as karma – what goes around comes around – but you don't know what form that's going to take. Don't do something for someone and then keep a scorecard. Karma may kick you in the backside then. Help others because it will make you a better person.

Another idea to help you maintain the servant attitude is to practice maintaining open lines of communication. As you're getting to know people, ask them for their input and ideas on things. Ask about how you can improve in your work or relationship with them. Understand their feelings – put yourself in that person's shoes. What is their life like – at work or home – and what can you do to improve it?

You must develop a willingness to put their interests and desires above your own. You will be rewarded with others who will go out of their way to help you. They'll also develop a desire to see you succeed in whatever path you take. That karma thing certainly helps!

Build Relationships

I'll spend a fair amount of time on this aspect of being a great follower. Out of all the characteristics I've mentioned so far - framing your goals, identifying strengths, being determined, showing initiative, and being a servant - building relationships might be the most important aspect of being a great follower. We need other people. It's as simple as that. They provide feedback and support, create opportunities and open doors. The majority of us will need to rely on someone else, at least a few times in our lives, to make our success a reality.

Now, for those of you who are naturally introverted, don't get too anxious. I don't mean that you have to be friends (or even friendly) with *everyone* in order to be successful. What is key is nurturing genuine relationships without expectation that you will get anything in return. That means traditional networking goes out the window. Gone are the days that you hand out business cards like crazy and only seek to garner a connection with someone to benefit yourself and your career. Your whole goal is to create a lasting, meaningful relationship with someone. This happens most naturally when you build on mutual interests.

How do you find those interests? Join a club that you're interested in. Make friends over hobbies. So, for example, if you're interested in golf, then certainly, bond over golfing. Don't golf just because everyone else is doing it. That's not beneficial. Your fellow golfers will be able to tell if you're not enjoying it and they will not trust your motivation for participating in the sport. For those introverts out there, if you enjoy reading, then you can join a book club. This is a great way to get involved.

The key is to be your authentic self. If you're being true to who you really are, you're going to find ways to network around what you're passionate about. Find like-minded people to interact with. You never know how that relationship will unfold in the future.

You could also start a new project at work that crosses departmental lines. Get involved in areas that you haven't been part of in the past. I know I recommended this to help increase your value to the company and your skills and experience. It's also a great way to begin your success journey because it covers so many points of being successful. You should focus on being as involved as possible. Get to know other people's jobs, the difficult parts and the easy parts. Get to know what the people on your team are interested in – both in their career and in their personal lives. Find some way to make a more meaningful connection. Put your servanthood trait to good use by finding out how you can help them with their success. Doing these things will open doors you never knew existed. You'll find great fulfillment in creating the network at your current employer.

Of course, you can always attend an event – whether it's specifically a networking event (which I personally believe doesn't work and can be a waste of time), or a conference of some sort. When you have an opportunity to chat with other people at these events, don't have small meaningless conversations. Spend more time with fewer people. Now, I don't mean latch on to one person and cling to them throughout the event. What you should do is listen effectively, participate in conversation and look for areas of commonality that you can develop relationships around.

You might need to brush up on your effective listening skills. Make sure you don't interrupt but give regular feedback that indicates you're listening by reflecting the other person's feelings. Also, if you do have a question, don't interrupt with your question. Wait for a pause. Finally, if the person you're listening to is presenting you with a problem, don't automatically offer a solution. Wait for them to ask – or if you feel you really have a great solution for them, at least ask them if they'd like to hear it before sharing. Once you've identified a couple of people that you share interests with, be sure to get their contact information so that you can follow up and start building a relationship with them.

If you're finding that networking really doesn't come naturally at all, you can set small goals around this activity. For example, make a goal to meet and talk to at least one new person a week. This doesn't necessarily need to be someone you've sought out to be part of your network. It could just be a stranger at the bus stop. You need to get in the habit of talking to someone that isn't part of your normal circle. Then, when you've developed that habit, you can more easily build deeper relationships around your hobbies or your job. You can't let fear determine your behavior. Ask yourself what's the worst that could happen if you talk to someone. Next, ask yourself, "Then what?" In other words, if the worst that could happen is that they could laugh at you, ask yourself, "What happens if they laugh at me?" You'll find that the 'worst thing' really isn't so bad after all.

Once you have a network, you can't rest on your laurels. You have to keep track of it and maintain it. It's helpful to make some sort of database – whether electronically or on paper – of your connections, how you're connected. Include their interests, birthday, family information – anything that will help you in keeping and building that relationship further. Then, be sure you are the one reaching out and keeping in contact. Don't wait for them and don't expect them to be the initiator. Of course, you should be thoughtful in how much you are contacting them. You don't want to be intrusive. Keeping the relationship going, however, is up to you. It's your network, not theirs.

I know that was a lot to take in. If you need to, go back through this chapter and jot down notes about those traits you could work on more. Determine if you need to adjust the goals you set earlier so that you can begin building on your success.

Chapter 6 - Learn More About Yourself to Find Your Best Fit

You need to figure out if your current strengths and way of thinking support the position you are in. And, to do that, you have to know what your strengths and unique perspectives on the world are. Strengths come in all sorts of guises. You could have different strengths in your personality. You could be naturally talented in certain areas. Your years of experience, your specific abilities to do certain things – these all add up to different aspects of you that can be translated to a successful fit in a career.

Many people struggle with seeing what their own strengths are. They may not know how to identify the difference between something they're truly good at or something they only *want* to be good at. They also have difficulty figuring out how to differentiate how they really are and how they want to be perceived. They might struggle with trying to understand how they can use the way they interact with the world around them in a unique way to be successful. Luckily for us, there are many, many tests and assessments available that will help us figure that out. You've probably heard about a few of these. They measure everything from personality types, to knowledge, skills and abilities, to natural talent. You can also take assessments that identify your natural inclination to different types of work. Let's review a few common assessments and look at how you can use them to find your strengths and support your success as a non-leader.

StrengthsFinder

CliftonStrengths® from Gallup is one of the more popular assessments used to determine a unique set of qualities in which you excel. This assessment is also known as "StrengthsFinder®." With this assessment, you complete an online tool where you select what you are more inclined to be like from a given pair of items. There are several options of reports available and you get varying degrees of information with each. I find the most useful is the CliftonStrengths 34, which gives you access to the entire assessment, rather than just your top five themes.

The word "themes" is used to describe the talents that we exhibit using a common terminology. Essentially, they group together certain behaviors that signify a specific talent into themes. Further, these themes are part of domains, which tell us how our talents align with certain aspects of working with others. These domains are relationship building, strategic thinking, executing and influencing. While the domains are geared toward leadership, I believe they are extremely useful for non-leaders, too. We all employ elements of these domains in our jobs – even if we aren't leading people. The domains in which your top ten talents land indicate how you might best contribute to a group, or team.

You may have noticed that I referred to "talents" quite often, rather than strengths. The CliftonStrengths assessment actually identifies your talents, not necessarily your strengths. So, what's the difference between a talent and a strength? Think about being naturally talented at a particular aspect of a sport – say you're very good at throwing a ball. Throwing that ball is just a talent. For that talent to be valuable (for you to perfect throwing the ball consistently in the way that you need to for your sport), you must practice and gain experience throwing the ball. This is how you make it a strength. So - like any natural talent that you have, you must exercise the aspects of your personality that come naturally to you to gain strength in it.

How do you use this to find a position that will be the best fit for you? Read the descriptions of your talents. Use the action plan suggestions provided in the book or on the website to advance those talents into strengths. For example, if one of your strengths is "Focus," you efficiently move toward your goals and stay on track. Of course, in doing so, you tend to be impatient with things that get in the way. So, one of the actions that you could take to advance your strength is to consciously pay attention when you think someone is going off on a tangent – what you would normally consider a "derailment." You might learn something. You could also work on limiting yourself to focusing on the projects with the highest priority so that you don't become frustrated with not giving each task the attention you'd like to.

Does your current role use the talents identified as your strengths? If not, look for job descriptions that might pick out certain words from your theme – strategic, for instance – and couple that with existing knowledge, skills and abilities to find roles that might be more suited to your talents.

You do need to be careful to use the results of your assessment in the way that it was meant to be used. The point is to spend your time and energy focusing on your strengths, rather than trying to fix those areas that might not come naturally to you. You also need to be aware that each of the talents has a challenge associated with it.

For example, one of my strengths is Competition. This means that I perform well when precise metrics are in place to measure my performance and there are goals for myself and my team to reach. On the flip side, I tend to always want to be at the top and seek to know where I stand. This can be exhausting! You have to learn what the challenging aspects of your talents are and put boundaries in place.

Further, know that the assessment does have a few negatives. For one, it works on the premise that you shouldn't spend time trying to fix your weaknesses. While, in theory, that sounds like a good idea, you can't always rely on your strengths to get your job done – nor can you always partner with someone who is strong in those areas.

Tom Rath, in the book *Strengthsfinder 2.0,* also claims that these talents can't be taught. So even if you wanted to work on the "talents" that aren't your strengths, you can't really make much headway, because these aren't learned skills. I have to disagree with that. If "positivity" isn't one of your top themes, but you are committed to becoming a person who gives out praise readily, you can learn to celebrate others' achievements, for example. No, you probably won't be as enthusiastic as someone who has this talent naturally, but you can learn to use it regularly with good results.

Finally, I believe that this assessment leaves out important "themes" of talent especially revolving around more creative or artistic talents. You might have a talent in understanding rhythm or movement – or even spatial organization. That's not addressed anywhere in the assessment and could be very useful for you when looking for an ideal fit for a job, or when you're looking to add more value in your role in your current job.

Myers-Briggs Type Indicator (MBTI)

Myers-Briggs Type Indicator (MBTI) is a tool that assesses your psychological preferences and how you see the world around you. It's based on Carl Jung's major orientation of personality. The initial assessment is on introversion and extroversion and three other basic functions of interacting with the world. These basic functions are stated as thinking or feeling, judging or perceiving, and sensing or intuiting (what we typically call intuition). The words that are used don't necessarily have the same meaning as you might understand them in common usage. For example, judging does not mean "judgmental." It means that you are planful and decisive. So, don't just take the nomenclature at face value.

When you take the assessment, you are given a four letter "theme" of how your personality comes through – there are 16 possible combinations. You may want to reference the full list at https://www.myersbriggs.org/my-mbti-personality-type/mbti-basics/the-16-mbti-types.htm.

These combinations come from your unique way of using the four functions – you could be **I**ntroverted, **S**ensing, **T**hinking, and **P**erceiving – giving you a "personality" type of ISTP. The theory is that you will always interact with the world and people around you in basically the same way because your personality is ingrained. That isn't to say that you will always get the same results every time you take the test, or that you are not flexible in how you respond. Because each of us use the four functions to a different degree, you may have only a slight preference for acting one way over another. Therefore, depending on the situation, you'll react differently.

You might also be thrown off by the overarching theme of how you interact with your world. These are identified as extroversion or introversion. Extroversion means that you put your energy (and feel energized from) interactions in the "outside" world. You get energy from people and things. Introversion, on the other hand, is when you get energy from the "inner" world – which are thoughts, ideas and images. The reason Myers and Briggs used those words is because they technically explain how those interactions manifest themselves in our lives. For example, if you interact with the world in an extroverted way, you feel energized being around other people. This doesn't mean that you are the "life of the party" all the time. It just means that you prefer to not be stuck in your own head.

Let's move on to the second set of functions. Sensing or intuition describe how we receive information. Sensing means that we are more comfortable and give more weight to information that comes through our five senses. If we can experience or have already experienced something, we'll rely on that more than we would an impression. Those who "sense" like to get information that is based on current, real information. Receiving information through intuition, conversely, means that you give credence to impressions or patterns. You have a lot of "what-if" thoughts going through your head. You don't mind dealing with the abstract or theories. In general, people are going to fall somewhere along the scale between the two. You'll use both sensing and intuition at various times, but you'll have a preference (whether slight or great) for one over the other.

The next set of functions deals with how you make decisions, whether logically ("thinking") or with your heart ("feeling"). Again, it doesn't mean that you will never make a decision using aspects of the other trait. Someone who lands with a preference on the "thinking" side of the scale will value impersonal facts over emotion, objectivity over harmony. Those who favor "feeling" are more concerned with how those decisions will affect the people involved, whether or not that's the logical decision.

Finally, the last set of functions deals with how you live your outer life. This can be judging or perceiving. As mentioned previously, judging deals more with being decisive, being structured, and being task oriented. Perceiving, on the other hand, is someone who is more spontaneous, and has bursts of energy – they take in information and organize around that, rather than needing the experience first-hand.

So, how do you use the information once you have it? You can decide if you need to flex how you're working. You can decide if your current position is a good fit for you. And you can determine what the challenges of your personality type are so that you can find things to work on. Let's tackle determining if the job you're in is a good fit.

Say you are an ISTJ type. You prefer to work with your own thoughts and ideas, not necessarily with other people. You use your senses when taking in information. You tend to make decisions logically and you are very task oriented. Currently, you're in a job that requires you to be very flexible with your schedule. You work with large groups of people all day long – and you have to make sure there is harmony in that team. Does that sound like a good fit for your personality? Probably not. No wonder you're miserable! You might be better suited to a role where you work on individual projects that you can base on previous experiences you've had and have a structured schedule in which you can plan your work. That sounds much more like an ISTJ position.

I'm not going to cover all 16 different types. You'll need to take the assessment to find out more about your specific type. There are multiple places you can take the assessment for free online. These work fine – at least on the surface. And, there is tons of information out there about each different type and what the challenges are for each in the workplace. It's ideal to take the actual assessment that's scored by a professional who is trained in the tool. You'll get a much more in-depth analysis of your personality type and how the information can be used in multiple areas of your life. This is an expensive route, though.

The tool also has a few deficiencies. One, it's based on your own perception of your personality. If you are not very self-aware, you may get results that aren't really a good reflection of who you are. Also, some people tend to answer the questions based on how they "want" to be, rather than how they really interact with the people and world around them. You have to be able to set aside how you'd like to be perceived and complete the assessment based on your first reaction (as that's generally the "real" you).

You also have to be aware that you are always going to be a combination of the different types. No one functions 100% of the time using only one aspect of personality. Of course, like any assessment, it should not be the only tool you use to help foster your success.

DISC
DISC is another assessment that measures your pattern of behavior. William Moulton Marston developed this theory in the 1920s. It measures what your tendencies and preferences are in specific situations. This particular assessment is very widely used in corporations – in fact, about 70% of Fortune 500 companies use this assessment as part of the hiring process. These organizations use the tool to assess how you would fit in the particular role you might be applying for and how you would mesh with the team. You can use it in a similar way - to find jobs that would work well with your particular preferences, and not be stuck in a job you would abhor because it goes against your very nature!

The assessment has four reference behaviors, which are **D**ominance, **I**nfluence, **S**teadiness and **C**ompliance. Dominance and Influence are considered "fast" behaviors – you like things moving, don't enjoy repetitive tasks and do well in environments of rapid change. Steadiness and Compliance are considered "moderate." People with a preference for these behaviors tend to enjoy calm environments with little change and don't mind doing things "by the book."

The other aspect considered with this assessment is people orientation versus task orientation. Dominance and Compliance are task-oriented, and Influence and Steadiness are people-oriented. Dominance, for example, is related to how you deal with problems, whether you are assertive and prefer control. Influence concerns the way you deal with people and how you communicate. Steadiness measures your temperament – to what degree are you patient, persistent or thoughtful. Finally, Compliance is your approach to activity and responsibility.

While a person taking the assessment will typically score higher in one behavior over the other three, they would never use that behavior in isolation. Just like with the other tools discussed, the behavior types are used in combination with one another. A person may even score fairly equally in two behaviors, showing they typically use those in combination.

Let's say my friend, Tina, took the DISC assessment. She scored high in Dominance, and she prefers positions that have some prestige and/or challenge associated with them. If Tina is secondarily high in Steadiness, she'll also want something that has a lot of standardization and will want to work in a calm environment that doesn't change much. As Tina did, you'll want to find jobs that use your unique combination of behavioral preferences more often.

Using this information about yourself will make it a bit easier to go into an interview armed with questions about what a typical day on the job would be like. Questions about opportunities for being visible in the company or department and the ability to work in an environment that is relatively calm would be important. Also, use the information to seek out special projects using your behavioral preferences that can enhance the value you add to the organization. Conversely, determine if a role is a poor fit by looking for environments or tasks that favor behaviors that aren't your preference. So, if you are not high in steadiness, a job that requires repetition would be boring to you. Instead, look for a work environment that frequently changes and has variety. These are things to look for before you get your foot in the door.

The DISC assessment is available for free from various websites online. You might have guessed – you get what you pay for. You typically will get at least your preference scores. Mine is Dominance 54%, Influence 22%, Steadiness 8% and Compliance 16%.... but I don't have information beyond that. To actually understand what that means and to interpret your unique pattern of behavior, you usually have to pay for an assessment.

There are several websites where you can purchase the assessment. The tool that has the most research behind it (backed by Wiley, the global publishing company) is from https://www.discprofile.com/. You'll know you're in the right place because their assessments are branded as DiSC (note the little "i"). There are several options, but I would recommend the tool that is for the workplace in general. You'll get the most use out of that particular report because its focus is broader than the other options.

Other Assessments

If those three weren't enough, there are plenty of other tools to help you find a good fit in the workplace. One that you might find very helpful is from O*Net, which is something that is offered from the United States government. You can find it at https://www.onetcenter.org/IP.html. This tool assesses your interests based on six types of occupational interests. Then, it will recommend jobs based on that and your level of education. It's definitely a step in the right direction, especially if you have absolutely no idea what types of positions your skills would be a good fit for. They also offer an "abilities" test, but that must be administered in-person at a job center.

I really like how the interests test combines what you like to do with what your skill set is. When you complete the test, you are given a list of best career matches and those that are considered a "great" fit – which is the next tier down from "best." Along with the career matches, when you click on each career, you get a profile of what it takes to be successful in that career along with the skills, education and personality profile that works well in that job. A sample profile is shown in the image.

Jennifer Raschig

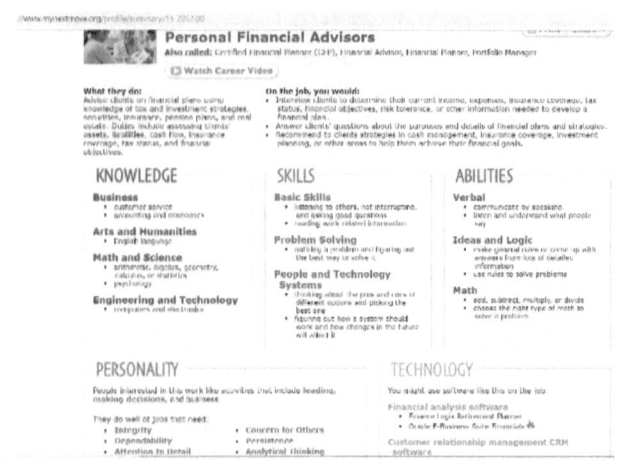

From "Personal Financial Advisors" by the National Center for O*NET Development. Used under the CC BY 4.0 license.

The interest test is absolutely free. You'll get all the information without shelling out money, unlike most of the other assessments. You can explore jobs based on the level of preparation or education required. It will match your interests and your level of current or future education and give you unique jobs based on that information. If you are interested in the abilities test, too, it would be in your best interest to do both the occupational interest and the abilities test at a job center so that you can get a complete profile.

Another career assessment that is widely acclaimed is the MAPP (Motivational Appraisal Personal Potential) career assessment. It's based on your motivations, along with your interest, personality, aptitude, work activities, and values. The test, consisting of 71 questions, doesn't take too long to complete. This tool is valuable in that, in a way, it combines some of the results you might have gotten from the other assessments into one test. The biggest problem, though, is that it only provides a very small sample of career matches for free. To really make good use of the time spent taking this test and for it to provide any real value, you'll need to pay for the results. The fee ranges from just under $100 USD to over $150 USD for the results, but I understand it's worth it if you are truly trying to find a new career that matches your unique personality, aptitudes and interests.

Putting your assessments to work

Of course, taking these tests is only valuable if the results are understood and put to use. To begin with, take one or two different assessments to get a feel for if you're in a position that suits your interests and strengths. Several of the tests offer insight into the types of jobs that would be a good fit for specific interests or personality types. It's possible to explore each of those alone and try to make some headway in finding a good match. Or, better yet, combine the results from several of the assessments to get more valuable information about where you'd be happy and where you could apply your strengths in a powerful way.

For example, Marcus took the Strengthsfinder assessment and found that his top five strengths are Relator, Competition, Strategic, Learner, and Input. Well, what does that really tell him? He would want to read the personalized assessment to understand how that would translate to success on the job. Then, he might take the MBTI test. Through this, he found that he is considered an ENTP personality type. He enjoys discussing innovative thoughts and finding new ways to do things. He's not afraid to play devil's advocate. When he combines his unique strengths profile with knowing that he enjoys being in an unstructured team environment where he can pursue new ways of doing things, he'll start recognizing jobs and positions that would be a great fit and allow him to use his unique skill set. You can do the same thing!

To take it even further, assessments like the MAPP are supposed to combine most of the different aspects of you as a total person, but it does it differently than the Strengthsfinder or the MBTI. If you're interested and don't mind spending some money, it would be worth it to get that insight, along with the list of jobs. What's really exciting is that you can then take that job list to the O*Net website and learn what you have to do to get into a job like that, what the outlook is and what the potential median pay is. And, of course, research jobs that would be similar.

Not ready to jump ship yet? You can apply the results to your current position. Think about how to turn your duties around or do them in such a way that speaks to your strengths. Possibly team up with someone else who complements your skills so that you are both successful. You will probably have to learn to sell the idea to your boss. If approached in a thoughtful way that shows how results will be provided, most often, you will be able to modify tasks to work in a way that provides better outcomes for the organization and yourself.

Have you taken any of these assessments yet? If not, consider stopping now and taking one or more of them to use in finding your best fit. Take time to think about what you can do with the knowledge you've gained through taking the assessment and how it can impact your work life. Then move on to learning how you can create engagement.

Create Engagement

Do you feel like you have low energy or no motivation a lot when you have to go in to work? Do you feel like you are absolutely drained at the end of the day – and not in a "I did a lot of great work" kind of way? What about the feeling of being stuck and you feel like you have no way out? These are all signs that you are not using your strengths, skills and natural abilities on a routine basis in your work. People who focus on their strengths are six times more likely to be engaged in their jobs and more than three times more likely to have overall life satisfaction. Isn't that what you want – life satisfaction?

Everyone goes through brief periods of feeling a lack of motivation or energy. What I'm referring to are sustained periods of time where you just can't get the energy to give 100% to your job. You rarely look forward to going to work. You don't have to feel that way. You need to find ways to become engaged in your work.

Engagement may be a new term for you – or it could be something you've heard tossed around, but you weren't sure how it applies to you in your work. Many people are confused on exactly what engagement is. According to Kevin Kruse, author of *Employee Engagement 2.0*, engagement is more than just being satisfied with your job. If you're satisfied, you'll go to work, you'll get done what's needed to get done (or what you're told to do) and you go home. You don't necessarily go beyond what is asked. Engagement is not about being "happy" with your job. Happiness doesn't go as deep as engagement. An employee can be happy because their company offers perks like a free gym membership, employee barbecues, or a nice vacation package. Those perks don't necessarily spur them toward engagement.

Engagement is an emotional commitment to your employer. You want what they want. The organization's goals are what you strive for. The engaged employee goes beyond what is asked and they do all they can to help the company reach its goals.

So, if engaged employees are more successful, what if you're not emotionally committed to your company? Ask yourself how you can attach what you are specifically responsible for, or what you choose to do outside of your responsibilities, to a broader meaning. Think about what the company does for the client in the end. How can that speak to you in a positive way? What are you helping them do? If you're hard-pressed to come up with something, look at your organization's mission statement. What purpose is the company fulfilling? That purpose is their ultimate goal. What is your specific role in making that happen? Even if you're the janitor or the administrative assistant who never interacts with a customer, you help the organization further their goals. Create your own meaning. Take ten minutes now to think about that. Write it down and look at it at least one time each day at work. Focus on your mission.

If the company's mission doesn't resonate with you, you'll need to redirect your energy on internal motivators to get and stay engaged. Generally, your internal motivators are not going to be related to money. Motivators have to be in line with your own personal goals. Money might be a means to achieve your goals, but it rarely is motivation enough to be emotionally involved in your job.

When you focus on those internal motivators, you're more likely to find success. Think about what you do in your job every day. What interactions do you have with the people around you, both clients and colleagues? What do you like or dislike about those interactions? Give those interactions that make you feel more motivated a lot of thought. What about when you're doing specific tasks? What challenges your commitment to the organization or what makes it easy to feel really great about the work you're doing? The answers to those questions are the things that are going to serve as internal motivators for you.

Another internal motivator might be a feeling of accomplishment – whether it's completing a project or learning a new task or concept. If you have a strength in competition, an internal motivator might be making a game of some of your duties and competing with yourself to get something done more efficiently or with better quality. An additional way to internally inspire an emotional commitment is increasing a competency, in your own duties or in something new that can be used to further the organization's mission. Or, aim for recognition as someone who is an innovator.

Conversely, figure out what things are demotivators for you and seek to change either your work or your perspective. What tasks sap your strength and energy? Are these assignments forcing you to flex outside of your basic personality style? For instance, are you performing a task that requires flexibility and spontaneous reactions, yet you prefer to have things scheduled? Think about how you can change the way you work, like maybe learning how to anticipate things and plan for them. Then you can create structure around that task. What about if you feel anxious about performing certain responsibilities or interacting with specific individuals? Ask why. In fact, keep asking why until you get to the root of the problem. Pay attention to the dialogue Greta has with a trusted supervisor to see how this works.

Greta said, "I don't like following up on these unpaid invoices."
"Why?" asked Jill, Greta's supervisor.

"When I follow up on the unpaid invoices, I have to deal with Mary at XYZ company because that company never pays on time."

Jill asked, "Why do you not want to deal with Mary at XYZ company?"

"Mary is extremely rude and uses foul language. She makes me feel like I don't know how to do my job," Greta responded.

Again, Jill asked, "Why do you feel like you don't know how to do your job?"

"Sometimes she finds errors in the invoices and refuses to pay – and I find that she's right… sometimes, anyway."

Jill persisted, "Why are there errors in the invoices?"

Greta stated, "The base price on the items they purchase from us is a variable amount in the system. Anyone can change that number."

For the last time, Jill asked, "Why can anyone change the number?"

"Some companies we do business with have different negotiated prices for that item," Greta said.

Jill responded, "Greta, this is the root of the problem. The solution would be to either have everyone pay the same price, or have parameters built in so that each company's negotiated price comes up accurately in the system. You will no longer dread following up on invoices with Mary because the invoice will be accurate more often."

This is a technique called "5 Whys." You may recognize this technique if you've studied the Lean approach to problem solving. Often used to find solutions to technical or process issues, you can also use it to solve your own workplace issues to make your job easier or more enjoyable.

Learn to focus on the company's purpose or mission and your personal motivators every day when you go to work. Use your strengths, your personality, your skills and abilities to come up with a new way to look at what you're doing. Concentrate on turning energy-draining aspects of your work into elements that, at the very least, are neutral to success. Then, you can focus on using your unique qualities to make you and your company successful.

Part 3: Your Organization, Your Leader, and You

Jennifer Raschig

Chapter 7 - Identify a good organization and leader/follower fit

There is more to personal success than the individual role you're in. The person you report to and the organization you are part of play a role in how you can be successful. Look for a position with an organization and with a leader that will allow you to enjoy success as you have defined it. So, actively look for roles that permit you to do that. This starts with the interview. But even before the interview stage, even before applying for a job, spend time thinking about your aspirations. Then, write down what you think you need to have in a job so that you are fulfilled and can achieve those aspirations. And, I do mean write it down! Writing those ambitions down makes them concrete. They are now more than a dream or a theory. Look at them every day to be reminded of your goals for your career. Even better, create a personal mission statement as a culmination of what you aspire to.

Interview for "fit"
Okay, now that you have a mission statement, and, based on the previous section, a good idea of your personal strengths, personality type and abilities, you can look for a position that aligns those things into a perfect fit. Be looking for an organization that really fosters the success of the individual person. Talk to people about the company. Read reviews on Glassdoor.com. Learn about its culture. Do all of this before you apply! Do as much pre-work as you can. You don't want to be in a situation where you are offered a position but have no idea if you'll like working there.

Once you've done your pre-work, you have a second chance to discover more information about the organization in an interview. An organization that nurtures individual growth will have some common characteristics. Knowing this, you can ask specific questions to find out where they stand. These companies will promote individuals from within first. This shows they support career development of their own employees and value the time that the person has invested with the company.

Growth-minded companies will also have a focus on training that other organizations do not have. This can mean an active training and education department within the company or some sort of benefit for education and training outside of the company's organizational development department. To find if a company is truly focused on the individual's growth, it's important to find out if it is promoting the career development opportunities it might have, rather than just providing skill training related to specific job roles. This will help you determine if they are interested in the whole person. Look for well-rounded education opportunities, not just on-the-job training.

Beyond those specific areas, you'll look for a cultural fit in general. What's important to you? Flexible schedules? Interaction among coworkers? Figure out what's important, then ask some questions that help you determine the company's culture related to that item specifically.

You won't get a great answer if you just ask, "What's the culture like here?" You'll need other questions that will reveal more than just the pat answer the previous question will provide. Think about things like, "What's the last major achievement the company celebrated?" This will tell you that the organization values success, and they recognize and call attention to it through celebration. It will also tell you what they consider to be a major achievement worth celebrating. You can dig further and ask about the department this position is in. What achievements have they celebrated recently and how was it celebrated?

Asking about the activities offered to employees could also be important. This can lead to insight about how 'together' the company expects employees to be. Do they expect you to like each other outside of work, or just work together? Neither way is wrong. However, you may prefer to leave your work relationships inside of work hours and have no desire to be a part of a company that really wants you to participate in the softball league during the summer months.

If you want to discover if you will be working on a team of real extroverts, you can ask what do the people on this team do for lunch every day. The answer will tell you if they socialize a lot or if they tend to do their own individual thing. This could be important to you if you want to socialize with your coworkers and find that they just aren't a friendly group.

Ask your interviewer how long they've been with the company. You generally want to hear that they've been with the company for quite some time, rather than a few months – unless of course you're interviewing with a start-up. You want to make sure there isn't a ton of turn-over because that's a big red flag that something isn't right with the company. If you've done your research ahead of time, you'll often be able to ferret out problem areas before the interview.

You'll want to find out how your success is going to be measured in the eyes of the leader. What and who determines your success? Is it the leader who determines you are successful, or someone else? What is the timeframe and how are those metrics established?

Finally, ask if the interviewer is willing to show you around the office. This is a fantastic way to get a feel for how things would be on a day-to-day basis. Are people interacting with each other? Do they have their cubicles or offices decorated? How is the lunch or break room? These areas are going to give you a big clue into what is valued at that office and the overall morale of the employees.

If the organization would be a good cultural fit, your next step in the interview is to determine if your direct leader will be a good fit for you. Leaders need to attract followers that possess the characteristics or qualities they want on their team. You'll know you're the kind of person they are looking for if you're attracted to their leadership style. You'll learn more about different leadership styles in chapter 9.

You can also look for an "eagle environment." According to John C. Maxwell in his book, *The 21 Irrefutable Laws of Leadership,* you want to look for an environment "where the leader casts a vision, offers incentives, encourages creativity, allows risks, and provides accountability." What he means is that a leader takes the broader view of what's going on, encourages you to handle your position and do your best work for the company, and provides a framework through accountability.

Find a leader who has a track record of developing other leaders. Even though the focus of this book is finding your own success outside of the leadership path, it's important that you work for someone who can and has developed leaders. Those leaders who have never fostered someone else's leadership growth tend to focus on their employees' weaknesses (rather than their strengths). They tend to treat everyone the same – because they want to be fair. You are not like the person in the seat next to you, and everyone's growth needs are different. So, find out by asking in the interview where team members who were previously in the department have progressed to. If there haven't been many people who have moved on to leadership positions, it could be a red flag that team members aren't being developed.

Overall, you should be evaluating each career opportunity through several lenses to get the best fit. Look for a job that promotes the sort of lifestyle that is important to you. Look at what the company values – what is its mission or vision statement? Does that resonate with you? Look at the cultural fit. Yes, at some point compensation does factor in, but priority should be given to lifestyle and job satisfaction (focusing on using your strengths and passions) when it comes to accepting a new position.

New Job, Wrong Role

Knowing how to interview for the best fit in an organization or with a new leader is one thing. But what if you just started a new job and you're now realizing that the person you report to is not the best fit for you as a follower? There are a number of things you can do, but they all lead to one important concept – increase your value to the organization as a whole.

It's important that you keep in mind that while you are working on increasing your value, you must get the work done that you were hired to do. You can't let that slide. Be sure to focus on doing your work. I do mean FOCUS. This means that you're not just doing something to get by. You really pay attention to what you're doing. You figure out how to do it more efficiently and with better results. Only once you've done this should you try to reach beyond your current responsibilities. You might find that there are certain aspects that you really enjoy, and you can use that to springboard into something else. Focusing will increase your value in the eyes of your boss and others' in the company.

You should always have a purpose in mind when you reach outside of your specific job duties. Set specific purposes or goals, if you will, so that you are looking for opportunities that reach those goals. Just like any goals that you set, you're going to want to set a long-term goal that is inspiring. Then establish and document short-term and mid-range goals to keep you on track. Begin working on the short-term objectives right away.

Proactively look for special projects and assignments that will allow you to attain additional skills beyond those that you use in your current role. This will not only increase your value to the company, but of course, will also increase your value when you're ready to move on to a new organization. The best way to go about finding a special project or assignment is to look for areas of the company that maybe aren't doing as well. Or, perhaps there is a big project that needs additional help. Ask to be put on that assignment. If you can do something using your unique strengths and abilities to help turn the company around, it can be a boost to your career. Others in the organization will take notice.

Once you have the attention of other leaders, there is a good chance that you can move into a role that might be a better fit for you. Remember, if you're looking to go beyond the scope of your current job, let your boss know what you're willing to do in exchange for the opportunity. Maybe you can ensure that certain tasks are done earlier than normal, or you can take responsibility for something else, easing your boss's burden. That will make them more inclined to allow you to venture outside your normal responsibilities.

Another thing to help increase your value, and therefore create a better fit in your new job, is to always be learning. You should be able to "describe what you've learned recently and what you plan to learn in the near future." And this includes knowledge, skills and abilities for future employability, according to Barbara

Moses, PHD, in her book *Career Intelligence – the 12 new rules for work and life success.* The goal when learning is to get good and stay good at tasks that use your talents and enthusiasm. You need to be sure to keep up with skills that got you the job in the first place, and then further them to include your abilities and new experiences.

If you're struggling with finding what to concentrate your education on, ask questions about where you can grow personally. This means not just concentrating on job duties or skills but going deeper to find out how to improve yourself overall. Consider what you'd like to transform in your life. Most people need to do a good deal of soul-searching to figure this out about themselves. However, you could look at the company you work for, or the job you're doing, and figure out what you'd like to transform there. Then, determine what skills or knowledge are needed to make that happen.

Always be looking to gain a broad repertoire of skills. An extensive skill set will make you more appealing to an organization. Even if you're not a specialist in most of those skills, just knowing about something can be helpful. For example, if you are a software engineer and have the opportunity to work on a project with an accountant, chances are, you'll pick up some of the terminology. You'll probably even understand a bit more about what they do. This basic knowledge could be important in a future role.

Another avenue to find potential growth areas is to ask your leader or others in the organization what would be valuable to them. You may be surprised at the answers they give and the opportunities available to you. Transformation can also come through finding someone who is exhibiting the behaviors you'd like to take on. Learn from them – if possible, form a mentoring relationship with them so that you have the arena to ask questions and gain some real insight.

A very compelling way to increase your value is to choose to help. Helping is always a choice. It goes back to one of the character traits of a good follower – that of "servanthood." You can choose to help in a number of ways.

One that stands out is to look for ways to mentor others in your organization. Usually this is a formal relationship, but you can also do it in an informal way. Find areas where you see someone may be struggling, where they lack the skills or knowledge to really do something well. If you have the knowledge, share that with them openly. I think people too often "hoard" knowledge because they think someone else will use that knowledge to get ahead of them. But, if you are seen as someone who will take the time to teach others and help them grow, you will grow immensely yourself.

There is a bit of a trick to share your knowledge without seeming to be a know-it-all. Your help will not be well-received if it makes the person you're interacting with feel inadequate. Use language that is directed inward, not toward the other person. Language such as, "What I found worked for me is…" Then, they can take your guidance or not. Maybe they've tried your way and it didn't work for them. Ask them if they would like some help before you just jump in. If you don't ask, they might resent your help.

You can always do something to help support your boss, too, even if you don't think their leadership style is a great fit for you. Look for little things that seem to fall by the wayside. Your leader may not have time to do those things. Or they may just prefer to do other tasks because it's not something that they enjoy doing or may not be easy for them. Even good leaders feel this way about some aspects of their jobs.

Sometimes, you can do those little things without asking permission; sometimes you need to ask before you take it on. You'll need to use your judgement. Your boss may take offense or may be very appreciative of your willingness to take some of the burden off of them.

Consider what can make their day easier, not what makes you stand out more. The goal here is to increase your value in their eyes – and you do that by easing their burden in a consistent way. When you do this, you may be given more opportunity to take on special projects or be on teams that fall outside of your normal duties but will increase your skills and experience.

Even if you aren't new to your role and you've been languishing for some time in a job that is a poor leader/follower fit, you can still make some changes. Again, go back to the assessments that you have taken. Search for areas of your job where you can really use your strengths, skills and abilities to move you further toward fulfilling your personal mission statement. You have to work towards that purpose so that the less appealing aspects of your job fade to the background. While you're doing this, actively search for a new position that will be a better fit for you and ultimately for your long-term success.

Chapter 8 - Communicating With Your Leader

Communication with the person you report to is key to attaining success, no matter how you define it. You may still be in a job where you're reporting to someone who isn't a good fit, but that doesn't matter. You will need to find a way to break past that barrier and communicate with them so that you can fulfill your role. And, of course, you want to communicate your own thoughts and ideas, not just be an echo of your leader. That is not being a good follower.

Align your goals

It's important to know what it is your leader needs to accomplish. Find out what their goals and objectives are. Then, seek to align your goals with theirs. (Remember, a successful follower knows what they want to accomplish; they understand their own goals.) Before going into a meeting with your boss, determine what you really want the outcome of the meeting to be. You should answer the question of "what do I want for me?" If you aren't clear about the desired outcome, you won't be able to move forward in a meaningful way. You'll be spinning your wheels.

Then, figure out what you want for your boss. In this case, the desire is for your boss to be able to meet his or her goals while letting you be successful. Maybe there's more to it than that. Depending on your view of life, or your view of your boss, you may want to accomplish more for them than just helping them fulfill their goals (which I talked about a bit in the last chapter). In either case, go into the meeting having a very clear idea of what you want the result to be for that person. Then, finally, know what you want for the relationship the two of you have together. Is it for the relationship to be built on more trust? Is there something else that needs to be fixed, or maybe an aspect of the relationship that can be grown? Focus on that when you head into the meeting.

Ask your leader what his or her goals are in a non-confrontational way in a meeting that is set aside for that purpose. You don't want to spring this question on them – especially if you aren't on great terms with them. It could come out as accusatory if asked in the wrong way.

Hear the difference in the way you ask. "Can you tell me what it is you're supposed to accomplish?" See how that can sound like maybe they aren't getting anything done? Contrast that with, "I've been thinking about how I can improve my performance and how I can help you more. I was wondering if you'd be willing to share your goals with me so I can align my goals to support you." This is a much softer way to ask and accomplishes what you want for you, for them, and for your relationship.

Let them know in your next one-on-one meeting that you'd like to discuss your goals and how you can help them fulfill their goals. Elicit their view on how they see your role fitting in to accomplishing their goals. Your leader may not have an idea of how you can help them immediately, but they'll go away thinking about it. And so will you. You have an advantage here because you are (hopefully) well aware of what you can bring to the table. You can find some way to use your unique set of strengths and abilities to help them accomplish their goal. Remember, the aim here is to move toward what you've defined as success – fulfilling your own personal mission statement through helping your boss achieve their goals.

Give and receive feedback

An additional element of communication to help in your success is the ability to give and receive feedback. It is a fallacy to believe that you only need to receive feedback and incorporate it into your job to learn and grow. You're not the only person involved in your job. Because everyone is impacted by those around them, we must also learn to give feedback to others in a constructive way that accomplishes a purpose.

Different types of feedback exist for different purposes. Let's focus on three different kinds. The first one is feedback in the form of appreciation. Appreciation is directed to a specific person. There is no ulterior motive in appreciation feedback. It's simply to let the person know you appreciate what they did or accomplished.

The next type of feedback is coaching or advice. You don't direct this at the person. Coaching is always geared towards the person's performance. And, yes, you can provide coaching or advice feedback to your leader. You just need to know how to deliver this in a way that the leader can accept it. I'll get to that in a minute.

The last type of feedback is evaluation. I think it's important that you understand that not all feedback is evaluation. Evaluation is basically comparing performances (whether to someone else's performance, or their own). When I talk about feedback through the rest of this section, I'll be referring only to coaching or advice feedback, not evaluation. It's not your job in a follower role to provide evaluative feedback. Your goal will be to help someone else improve or succeed. You can't do that with evaluation feedback.

When you are looking for feedback for yourself, you're showing that you have a desire to improve or seek new ideas. You give off the vibe that you are open to change and that you can take constructive feedback. Don't wait until an annual review. You should be seeking constructive comments about your performance throughout the year – in many situations and from people other than your boss.

Be clear in what you're asking for, as you might get comments that are off the mark. Let's see this in action.

Deanna asked for feedback from her boss because she felt like she was struggling with having her ideas heard in meetings. She talked with Frank beforehand and asked him to watch for times that she did speak, or when she should have spoken up, but didn't. And, she asked him to talk with her afterwards to let her know how she could improve. After the meeting, Frank let Deanna know that he felt like she spoke up a few times but didn't do well in getting her point across. While this was good feedback, it didn't help Deanna because it was too general.

This may happen to you, too. Don't let the person providing feedback get away with generalities. Ask for specific examples of what you did well and what didn't work. In Deanna's case, when she pressed Frank for examples, he let her know that when she spoke up about the budget shortfall, Sam from accounting immediately talked over her as if she'd never said a word. That's much more valuable feedback for Deanna as she can be listening for it and work on interjecting to be heard.

Now, depending on who is providing the feedback, they may not be able to give advice on how to improve the problem. However, once you understand the areas you need to improve, there is a good possibility that you can work independently to find ways to overcome the deficit. If it's your boss providing the feedback, seek their guidance on what you can do differently the next time.

Also, don't let time pass between the time they are observing you and the time you are getting the feedback. The more time that passes, the less they'll remember specific examples to give you. So, at the time you ask them to observe, be clear that you need time with them immediately after the observation for feedback. It doesn't have to be a long, drawn-out conversation. It can be a quick two- or three-minute chat. Just make sure it's immediate.

Other ways to ask for feedback are questions like, "If you had to make two suggestions for improving my work, what would they be?" Or, "How could I handle ___ more effectively?" When receiving the feedback, don't become defensive, make excuses or explain things away. Don't comment at all, other than to ask a clarifying question or two. You need to take the time to really hear and absorb what the person has to say. Let them know you appreciate their honesty, and that you need time to think about what they've said. Then, set aside time to ponder their words and create an action plan around the feedback.

Giving feedback is just as important as receiving it. As you give honest helpful feedback, you'll build better, more trusting relationships – which will help further your success. Have a goal or purpose in mind before providing the feedback. Efforts to "help" someone with their weaknesses will not be appreciated, especially if a relationship of trust hasn't been established. Pointing out a colleague's opportunities for improvement should never be about building yourself up, either. Just as in the conversation with your leader about understanding their goals, think about why you're giving the feedback. Before the feedback conversation, you'll want to discover what you want for yourself, the other person and the relationship.

You should also make the receiver of the feedback feel safe. Humans tend to view feedback (especially negative feedback) as a threat to their safety. This triggers the "fight or flight" response. If we don't feel safe, we're going to either get defensive or leave. Essentially, we're not open to anything you have to say because we don't trust you to keep us safe.

You must build the relationship up to the point that the receiving person trusts that you will not harm them and realizes that the goal is to build them up. You can't jump in with, "You handled that wrong." Notice and communicate the things they are doing well and provide appreciation feedback first. Bring in the advice feedback later. No, you don't always need to use the "criticism sandwich." The criticism sandwich is when negative feedback is provided sandwiched between positive statements about that person or their work. "The presentation you gave today was really great. You put a lot of work into that. (*Positive*). I don't think you handled the questions about the project timeline very well. You weren't prepared to speak to any of their concerns. (*Negative*). But, overall, you kept the meeting on track. (*Positive*)" That could backfire because it's not usually done well, and the positives are almost always not genuine. People sense the negative coming and they focus on that. So, be genuine in any feedback you give, positive or negative, and provide enough appreciation feedback that the person trusts you.

Once you know why you want to provide the feedback, then ask permission to share it with them. If the person isn't open to hearing what you have to say, it will do no good and will probably harm the relationship much more than it will help the relationship. The way to ask if they are willing to hear feedback is by saying something like, "I noticed (insert behavior here). Would you be okay with me sharing my observations with you?"

Remember, coaching feedback is directed toward the activity, not the person. Depersonalize the feedback. Focus on the task or action and seek to understand what they are trying to accomplish.

You might begin with "If you are trying to (insert task or outcome), here's an idea that might help." That person may not be trying to accomplish what you think they are. Phrasing the feedback in this way gives the person an opportunity to correct you and ultimately lead to a better understanding.

Another approach is to extend their successes. This is similar to appreciation feedback but has a coaching element to it. Rather than focus on the negative, your focusing your attention on getting the person to do more of the positive action. You can even do this with your boss. You can help them be more open to feedback by suggesting that their employees are looking to them to see how they act. The employees may be more open to giving and receiving feedback with each other if they see their leader doing the same. Then, use similar strategies that you would with a colleague. Appreciate what they do, model the behavior of asking for feedback, and build a relationship of trust to make it safe for them to be open to hearing feedback from you.

By the way, if you want to be more than a "yes" person, this is the way to do it. Building the trust in the relationship will allow you to share opinions and ideas that differ from your boss's viewpoint. And, because they trust that you have the organization's interests at heart, based on your previous conversations and feedback, they'll be likely to listen to what you have to say.

Teach your boss to manage you

Communication goes beyond feedback and goals. For your success, clue your leader in to how to effectively manage you. This is, in part, coaching your leader while asking for feedback, but it's much more than that. You also need to communicate your expectations in your role and working relationship with your boss.

Now, it probably won't work to just say, "I expect you to have weekly meetings with me where we discuss my projects and my goals." What could work is letting them know that you do your best work when you have regularly scheduled check-ins with them. It's all about the phrasing. You probably aren't in a position to make demands but communicating to your leader what works best so you can give your best performance will be advantageous for all involved.

Something else that helps your boss lead you is to teach them how to be more definite in their instructions. For example, if you're asked to prepare a report, keep asking questions until you know exactly what they want – and when they want it. Sometimes you have to fill in the blanks yourself. However, if you're someone who needs clear direction, you have to take the initiative to get it.

Deadlines especially are something that leaders often leave out, unless it's super critical. But, having a deadline helps you to plan your work. If you're not given one, take the time to figure out from your supervisor what their expectation is. Even if they didn't have anything in mind, press (in an assertive, but non-threatening way) until you get one. Just let them know that you would like to make sure you're prioritizing your work appropriately and having a due date would really help with that.

When communication is non-existent or breaks down

As you know, communication is a two-way street. To have effective communication, you will likely need to flex your communication style to meet your leader's preferred style. It's helpful to focus on your leader's intent and figure out whether they are more often focused on people or focused on the task at hand. Knowing these two parameters and whether they are typically passive or aggressive will enable you to flex how you're communicating with them. Changing your communication style to mirror your leader's style can also be helpful to diffuse situations that may have escalated.

Knowing the leader's intent is important. In general, people communicate with one of four outcomes in mind, according to Drs. Brinkman and Kirschner in their book, *Dealing With People You Can't Stand*. (I highly recommend this book, by the way.) They want to get it done, get it right, get along or get appreciated. Normally, the goal of the communication is balanced. For example, the goal may be to "get it done," but it will probably be balanced with getting it done correctly while getting along with others. Under stress, however, we typically focus on only one intent.

How your leader communicates with you will depend on their intent and their focus – whether it's on people or tasks. When we put it all together, we end up with ten different styles of communication. Now, when you and your supervisor have the same priorities – whether it's to get a task done, or to get along – then there usually isn't a conflict. Miscommunication arises when you have a different priority.

There are some techniques to help with establishing effective communication. First, you have to find common ground. As stated in *Dealing With People You Can't Stand,* "Success in communication depends on finding common ground before attempting to redirect the interaction toward a new outcome." A helpful tool to use when creating common ground is blending. You probably use blending already and just aren't aware of it. Blending comes in many different forms.

One form of blending is changing your rate of speech and intensity to match your supervisor's speech pattern. You might have heard previously that to calm someone down or diffuse a situation, you should speak in a quiet, slow manner. That's not exactly true. It would only diffuse a situation if the person that you're trying to communicate with is speaking in a quiet, slow manner. Otherwise, that person will have the impression that you just don't get how upset they are. You not only need to match the volume, but you also need to speed up your rate of speech and use words and phrasing that increase the intensity of what you're saying.

Blending also means mirroring body posture and other nonverbal behavior. Be careful, though. Don't overdo the mirroring to the point that it's noticeable to the person you're communicating with. They could believe you are mimicking them and that will destroy any rapport you might have built up. It might help you to observe people in conversations to see the mirroring process. Then, if possible, practice mirroring with someone that you trust will give you good feedback. They will be able to tell you if you're mirroring naturally or if you're doing it so much that it seems to be mocking.

After you've begun building rapport through blending, then you can start turning the focus to a more positive outcome. The goal of communicating is either to understand someone else, or have others understand you. Always try to listen and understand your leader before trying to have them understand you. The best way to understand is to ask questions for clarification.

You can also restate things they've said to make sure you've understood. This, of course, is not repeating their words back at them verbatim, but in your own words repeating the important points. Using the clarifying and restating techniques to recognize the person's intent and acknowledge it helps to move toward a positive outcome. So, if your leader's core intent is to get appreciation, you could open up dialogue more if you candidly (and genuinely) expressed gratitude for something they've done. This action will allow them to be more receptive to true dialogue.

Being understood is the second part of the equation. Just as you worked to understand your leader's intent, they need to know you have good intentions as well. So, if they've disagreed with a request you've made or with how you plan to go about a task, stating the intent behind the action will help them understand. In turn, it provides an opportunity for them to suggest alternatives to achieve your intent within the framework they had in mind.

Communicating with your leader encompasses a lot more than just a conversation here and there. Understanding their goals so that you can align what you are doing to support them in their achievements is key. Your success in many ways depends on their success, so be sure you understand how they see your role impacting them.

Ask your leader and colleagues for feedback. Take time to absorb what they have to say and apply it to move toward your goals. Look for opportunities to provide feedback to your leader and to your colleagues. Do this in the spirit of helping them achieve what they want, rather than moving yourself forward.

You can also teach your leader to manage you towards your idea of success by letting them know what will be helpful for you to be the best employee possible – whether that's through having regularly scheduled feedback sessions or communicating deadlines to help you set priorities. It all goes back to the principles of good communication – listening to understand and speaking to be understood. Understand their intent and communicate your own so that you can move to common ground and ultimately to success.

Chapter 9 - Flex to Match Your Leader's Style

Yes, there are different leadership styles. And, yes, to reach your definition of success, it's helpful to understand the different styles and how you can adapt your ways of working and communicating to mesh better with your leader. Think about how different leaders who like everyone to participate in decision making are from leaders who just lay down the law and expect you to follow. You would need to adapt to each of these styles to work effectively with them. Of course, it will also clue you in to if this is a good leader/follower dynamic for your goals.

A great deal has been written about leadership styles and there are many schools of thought about how many there are. The five different styles referred to in this chapter are a culmination of the research on the topic. Read on to learn some pointers on how to navigate each leadership style and how to adapt your "follower" style so you can be successful.

Autocratic Leader

Autocratic leaders, also known as authoritative leaders, are direct and decisive. There is rarely discussion about decision making. Autocratic leaders that ask for input do exist, but they seldom rely on that input for making changes or decisions. Orders are given and expected to be followed. You will recognize this type of leader by the very clear expectations laid out for you. You will rarely be asked for your thoughts or opinions on anything. These leaders tend to trust very few people and will infrequently delegate to anyone outside of their small trust circle.

While this type of leadership may rub many people the wrong way, it is quite effective in several situations. In fact, it's important in work environments like the military, or in production work, where adhering to regulations is extremely important and there is only one right way to do the job. Autocrats can also be very effective when they are appointed as a group leader to assign tasks and set deadlines.

You may have problems in this relationship if you have difficulty adhering to strict rules, or if you prefer to find the most innovative way to go about a task. You may have to flex out of your creativity at work or think very long and hard about your idea before sharing it with your supervisor. Your idea could very well be something that has merit and will work better than current methods, but you'll need to be able to prove that in a logical, well-reasoned way. You don't have to always agree with your boss, but you do need to be extremely thoughtful and thorough if presenting a dissenting argument.

In general, you'll want to keep this leader informed of where you're at in a project or task, but not necessarily the specifics of how you arrived at that point. This leader will quickly become impatient with hearing the minutia, but they do not want to be surprised. They need to be in control and so knowing any significant issues or successes will be important for them.

Keep in mind that this type of leader is focused on the intent of getting the task or project done and likely, getting it done right. They aren't going to be focused on getting along. So, you'll need to remind yourself that the blunt feedback you receive is not personal. They are not attacking you personally. This is probably one of the more difficult things to recall if you're working for an authoritative boss. Know that they will hold you accountable for your work and expect you to take responsibility.

Now, not all autocratic leaders forget there is a human element involved. There are leaders that have learned to recognize when you've done your job well and can reward successes. So, don't automatically think that this relationship won't work simply because you recognize that your boss wants to be in control of all situations at all times. You may find that you can get into their circle of trust by taking ownership of your responsibilities, doing your job to their standards and speaking up appropriately in a well-thought-out manner.

Laissez-Faire Leader

If you're not familiar with the term, laissez-faire translates literally from French as "allow to do." With the laissez-faire leader, you'll have a lot of freedom in how you do your job. This leadership type is the opposite of the autocratic leader. While the autocrat controls everything, the laissez faire leader has really no control over decisions and how things get done. They should provide the supporting framework – the vision – of where the department or organization is going and provide the resources to make it happen. They rely on their subordinates to figure out how to get it done. That doesn't mean that they don't know what's going on, but they don't actively step in and provide direction.

They will give advice and support when asked, but they trust their employees to make the right decisions and do the best work they can for the company. Ultimately, while they don't make the decisions, the leader is still accountable for the result of their employees' work. This means they need to setup sufficient system of reward or disciplinary action to incentivize employees to get the job done well.

If your leader is one who is very hands-off and doesn't give you any direction, you probably have a laissez-faire leader. As you can imagine, this can lead to chaos if the leader doesn't hire the right people to get the job done. This boss can be a difficult one to work for if you ultimately need someone to take control and make the hard choices. If you need to have deadlines to work toward or someone giving you the procedures to get the job done right, you will struggle under this person's leadership. For a good laissez-faire leader, their ultimate goal is to see people find the right direction on their own. They want to foster growth, be a mentor and allow people to find their own path.

If you find yourself working for a laissez-faire supervisor, set your own procedures if you need them. Consult with colleagues on the best way to do things. Write the procedures up for yourself. Be sure to set yourself deadlines, too. You don't necessarily have to communicate to your leader that you've taken these actions because the point is to create structure for yourself. Volunteer to create structure for others. This will further your skills and experience so that whenever you are ready to move on from this position, you can demonstrate that you have the capability to organize the job in a logical and effective way.

Your leader will want you to come to them for advice, though. So, if this isn't something that you've done frequently in the past, get accustomed to using them as a sounding board. Also, you'll need to be very comfortable communicating what resources you need to get the job done well. If you don't know what you need, talk with others in similar positions, or perhaps find mentors in other businesses or industries that can help you figure that out. Remember, there aren't rules, so you'll have quite a bit of freedom in determining the best way to go about getting your job done.

Transformative Leader
You might recognize a transformative leader by their inspiring vision. These leaders motivate their employees through passion. Working for this person, you'll be able to see the big picture. They are adept at communicating the vision of where the department or company is going, but they don't concern themselves with the day-to-day details of operations. Your transformational supervisor will be very interested in your individual contribution so they can recognize you for the role you've played in the team's success.

This type of leader is very successful in departments or organizations that have employees that are skilled in their roles and in industries that are not highly regulated – allowing for creativity in how employees carry out their function. This leadership type is especially useful when a department or company is going through change. Because the person is so inspiring, they can unite employees to a common cause and make great strides in moving the organization forward. A transformative leader sounds like they would be the ideal person to work for – inspiring, interested in your individual part in the process and encouraging creativity. Issues can come up in a few areas, though.

If the transformational leader does not constantly keep up with communicating the vision, employees can lose interest and become disengaged. Because this leader is not typically concerned with the details of how to carry out the vision, employees may not be successful in achieving results. Employees may feel pushed to achieve beyond what is reasonable and experience burnout more quickly than in other organizations.

So, how do you adapt if you work for a transformational leader? Identify if you need additional organizational planning or detail to carry out your job function. Because your leader will be interested in your individual input, approach them with ideas you have regarding how to carry out your work. Press them a bit for detail or ask about written organizational plans. They may have tasked someone else with that responsibility. You could also create your own plan starting with the vision, then working backward to your starting point. Brainstorm with others to fill in the detail, if needed. You'll need to have strong organizational skills, but this experience will be very helpful to you now and in future roles.

If you feel like you're being pushed to give more and more, and are feeling burned out, set personal boundaries. You have to decide that balance is more important than fulfilling a supervisor's unrealistic goals. You may be questioned about your commitment. Have a plan in place for how to achieve what is requested, but within your boundaries. The great thing about a transformative leader is that in general, the end result is what matters. If you can get to where you need to be, along with everyone else, then it doesn't matter that you aren't burning the candle at both ends.

Transactional Leadership

Rewards and punishments are the hallmarks of transactional leaders. They rely on extrinsic motivations through the use of reward systems – which is different than transformative leaders, who inspire you to be intrinsically motivated. Transactional leaders, also referred to as "management" leaders provide clear structures with controls in place to achieve reachable short-term goals. They do allow some independence in choosing how to go about doing the work, as long as it is within the boundaries of the rules and structure put in place. If you work for a transactional leader, you will find they tend to get results through processes that have been proven to work. They are not often innovative or creative in how things are done.

This type of leadership works well for companies that are well-established. The organization is not in an era of growth and therefore, being creative or coming up with new ways of doing things is not expected of management. Often, employees of a transactional boss feel like the leader doesn't care about them personally. For this type of supervisor, it's all about the processes and the results. There is rarely consideration given to the employee's emotions. You may feel stifled under this type of leadership if you enjoy coming up with solutions to problems, or you enjoy finding more efficient ways of doing things.

To ease your working relationship with a transactional leader, keep your conversations with your boss focused on the task at hand and results, as they will have little time for personal conversation. If you feel like there could be more efficient ways to perform your role, create a structure or plan and present it to your boss with anticipated actions and results. Even if your leader doesn't agree with you moving forward with the new idea, you've at least planted the idea that something new could work. Because this leader is focused on results and structure, they could potentially try your idea. You may not be recognized for it, but you will have the satisfaction and experience to add to your resume.

Participative Leadership

Participative leadership is also known as democratic leadership. The defining characteristic of this style is that employees are asked for their opinions and ideas and the group makes the decision, rather than the leader. There are multiple variations of the participative or democratic style, all with varying degrees of employee participation in decision making, but this book will focus on the definition given above. Collaboration and teamwork are encouraged. The leader should be a great communicator and keeps employees informed of everything so that sound decisions can be made.

This particular kind of leadership has often been touted as ideal for many situations – especially in organizations that have complex issues that need to be solved. Because so many people are bringing their ideas to the table, the best solution can often be found and implemented. Participatory management inspires creativity. Employees remain committed to the organization because they can see their ideas are heard. They can make a real difference in what happens in the workplace. And, because the environment is so open and collaborative, there is very little competitiveness compared with what you might experience with other leadership styles.

Democratic leadership can fail when not executed correctly. Your leader may not be a great communicator. Decisions will then be made without all the information. Sometimes, the democratic process takes too long. Because this manager is looking for everyone to participate and have input into the decision, it is difficult to be nimble in a rapidly changing environment. Some participative leaders may be reluctant to take responsibility if the decisions aren't made timely, or if it was a poor decision. Because the group made the decision, it would be easy enough for them to lay blame. While that's not good leadership, it is a potential pitfall of this leadership style.

Working for a good participative leader is usually smooth sailing. Some people, however, may be uncomfortable participating in an open forum, or having a hand in the decision-making process. If this is the case, consider voicing your opinion to your leader in private. They are interested in knowing what you think. Because the goal is to choose the best ideas to implement, they want as many opinions as possible to get to the group for decision making. You can, most of the time, choose not to participate at all, and leave decisions up to your co-workers. Your boss might demand that you participate. Make a point, then, of speaking up and contributing to the process. If possible, explain to your supervisor that you are quite comfortable with your co-workers' ideas, and that you'd like to get involved in other ways. That way, you are not seen as being disengaged. You can use your talents elsewhere.

Even if the leader is a great democratic boss, you might be longing for a bit of competition in the workplace to motivate you to do more. This might be one of your strengths. You may need to flex to more internal competition. Set higher goals for yourself. Or, talk with your leader about projects or tasks that would be a stretch for you.

If the leader isn't a good democratic leader, they could be avoiding any decision making at all and waiting for the team to always point them in the right direction. They could also not take responsibility for failures. If this is the case, document decisions made and the information the decisions were based on. You could even take your documentation further by noting the outcome of the decision and what you might have done differently next time. Use this for experience in other roles that you might be preparing for. A bad participative manager is difficult to work with for very long because most employees can't tolerate the indecisiveness or the blame.

Leaders Flex Their Style

Most leaders flex the way they manage according to the situation. While this chapter reviewed each type individually, the best leaders use a combination of different styles appropriate to the state of the organization, the needs of the department and the mix of employees in the department. They will recognize when inspiration is needed to motivate employees to move through change. They will provide structure for the department and standard rules to operate within. A great manager will allow employees the freedom to be creative and encourage their growth. Rewards and discipline will be used when necessary. In the end, the best leaders realize they are responsible for the results of the department and organization and will make the best decisions based on the information available and input from the employees.

It is helpful, though, to recognize what style your leader is currently using. If you're struggling with their leadership, you can use the information in the chapter to identify what the leader's mindset is. Then, you can adapt how you're following so that you can continue to move toward success.

Part 4: What's Next

Jennifer Raschig

Chapter 10 - Moving in, out, here, and there

A multitude of opportunities await you once you determine your strengths, personality preferences and what type of leader and organization you want to work for. You need to be clear about what you want your success to be. This was discussed at length towards the beginning of the book. Now is the time to create areas of focus so that you can identify the best opportunities for you.

Current Skills Assessment
So, if you're not moving up – at least into leadership – let's define how you're going to move. First, assess your current skills. Spend some quality time really thinking about this. Ask others what they feel your top skills are – whether it's a boss, coworker or family and friends. Moving in your role could be expanding on those skills. So, if you are good at organizing and managing your time, for instance, what can you do to expand the use of those skills in your career? Maybe you look into roles that include more project management. As you might recall, taking on additional work that uses your top skills that are outside of your normal job description is a great way to potentially transition from a job you don't like into something that is a new career.

When you're doing your assessment, don't forget to include skills you use outside of your current role. That's why it's important to ask friends and family. They'll have a different picture of who you are than your colleagues. People who know who you are in your personal life and have seen you engage in hobbies and other passions outside of work will be able to provide insight into your "whole" being.

Don't just think about your skills – make it concrete by writing it down! Writing the information down will help you rank your top skills and activities that you really enjoy. You could even make a spreadsheet (if you're really into it) and include such things as an "Energized?" column. See the example spreadsheet shown. This exercise will be beneficial as we move forward with setting goals, which is the next step to moving into a new role.

Skill	Current Skills		Ideas for Future Usage
	Used in Current Job ?	Feel Energized When Using?	

Current Skills Spreadsheet

Set Concrete Goals

Once you have identified those skills you feel energized using and would like to include in your next job, set goals around moving into that next position. So, using the example of becoming a project manager – that's your end goal. What are your short and mid-range goals to get there? Your short-term goal is to find two projects outside of your normal scope of work that you could take the lead on. Your mid-range goal could be to find and begin a project management certification course.

Again, it's important to write the goals down and to make them SMART goals. If you need a refresher on SMART goals, review chapter 5. The point is to build on your skills assessment to create your goals

Find a Mentor

It can be very helpful to have a mentor on this journey with you. While you may have a good sounding board with a friend or former boss, the relationship between you and a mentor is a formal one. You could very well turn an existing informal connection into a mentoring partnership. Both parties do need to be clear on that, as it is a commitment of time and energy.

To find a mentor, first, turn to who you know. In general, it is easier to begin with someone who is at least familiar with you and your work. Identify people from your network that have the qualities you aspire to. Learn more about their background and experiences so that when you reach out to them about a more formal relationship, you have something to build on.

While it is ideal to engage a current member of your network as a mentor, it isn't always prudent. If you want to move into a different industry, the best course may be to seek out someone outside of your normal channels. Use LinkedIn to find someone who may be in the role that you want to ultimately land in. If you can, message them explaining that your goal is to be in a similar career. Ask if they would be open to spending 30 minutes with you to answer some questions about their career. Be sure to be prepared for that meeting by finding out as much as possible about their background so that you can ask appropriate questions. You don't want to squander the opportunity with the potential mentor, so be on time and dress professionally. Asking them to mentor you in this first contact would certainly be a faux pas. You need to take the time to cultivate the relationship. Reach out occasionally – do what you can to help and support them before asking any more of them.

If you're uncomfortable reaching out to someone in this way, spend time networking through different forums. Join a group that is focused on the industry you want to be in. When possible, review membership lists and find people in roles that you aspire to. Participate in the group – don't just go through the motions. Not only will you connect with your future mentor, but you will also learn from everyone else and gain recognition with others in the industry.

Once you establish a mentoring relationship, let them know your goals, the assessments you've done and what you consider growth. The right mentor will have great insight into how to go about moving into the right position. You have to do the work, though! Don't just listen to what they have to say. Take the advice and act on it. I'm not saying that you have to do everything they recommend, but don't ignore their wisdom. You spent time choosing this person for their knowledge, so don't waste it.

A good mentor will also have you reflect on your own growth and actions needed to get where you want to go. If you haven't already done that work, they often will ask probing questions to help you understand your growth and your end goal. They'll help you gain clarity about your next steps in the form of short- and mid-term goals.

Change Your Behaviors

If you've discovered where you want to go, but realize your work habits don't support that role, don't despair! It turns out, you can teach an old dog new tricks. If possible, get your hands on a job description of the type of position you want to be in. The job description will give you a lot of information about what experience you need to have, and it will also likely give you behaviors that the hiring leader is looking for in that role. Of course, the job description is probably not going to have a section titled "Behaviors," but it usually has something that highlights the skills and proficiencies needed. Behaviors are often found in that area of the description.

Let's see this in action. Scott has completed a certification in project management and he's looking to move into that field. He knows he still has a few areas to work on before he can obtain a position as a project manager. He started reviewing job descriptions and noticed that they list verbal and written communication, collaboration and attention to detail as proficiencies wanted in potential candidates. These are all behavioral skills that can be learned.

When Scott reviewed these behaviors, he realized that he could really work on his communication skills and collaboration. If this happens to you, don't try to change behaviors in several areas at once. Choose one skill to work on. In Scott's case, he chose to work on communication skills.

Make sure you're specific about the behavior. "Communication skills," for example, is very broad. Scott will need to narrow his focus to a particular communication skill, such as listening. Once you've decided on a specific, narrowed behavior, you'll want to set some goals around changing or improving that behavior.

Remember, goals need to be SMART (specific, measurable, attainable, relevant and timely). For Scott, he could say specifically that he's going to improve his listening skills by not interrupting the speaker while they are talking. Then he could ask a trusted colleague or his boss to take note when he does that in conversation, so that he can measure improvement. And, he can set a time frame around improving that behavior.

When you do this, be sure to put those newly acquired behaviors to work. Look for opportunities that require specific behaviors. If you've worked on your collaboration skills, for example, find a task that allows you to work with and depend on someone else. Practice in smaller arenas and slowly work your way up to using those skills in bigger projects.

Take note of projects or work situations where you've used that behavioral skill. You'll appreciate having that documentation when interviewing for positions that require that proficiency. Many employers now do behavioral interviewing where they ask for you to elaborate on a time when you used a specific skill and what the result or outcome was. Because you've done research on the job description and have focused on developing those behavioral skills in particular, you should have very specific examples to use.

Chapter 11 - Asked to Lead

You've done really well in your job and you are seen as an expert. A new position has come up and your leader is strongly encouraging you to apply for the role. But – you know in your heart that being a leader of people in a position of authority is not what you want, or where your strengths are. So often, high performers such as yourself are asked to move into these management positions, but it's not the best thing for your career. Alternatively, you could be feeling like you've done what you can in your role and have exhausted opportunities for additional one-off projects that would expand your skills and experience. Now you're feeling like you're ready for more. So how do you deal with this?

Create your own job
It's going to be hard to reject that push to be a people leader but talk with your supervisor about possible solutions. One answer might be to help your leader create a position with similar duties, but without people management responsibilities. This will probably require a larger organizational change than most companies are willing to make, but it's definitely worth exploring.

Another answer would be to find out why your manager pegged you for the leadership role. See if you can expand your role to include more responsibilities in those areas, rather than moving into the supervisory position. Typically, this solution would entail keeping most of your current responsibilities and adding to them. Job roles are created all the time in these scenarios. It won't happen, though, unless you ask.

If you're the one feeling restless and in need of a change, approach the problem from a different perspective. You don't necessarily need to leave the company. Just like you might have been doing when you were looking for projects to expand your skills or network, take another look around the organization. This time, you're looking for ongoing business needs that have not been addressed, and that match your skills, strengths and aptitudes. Then, create a plan, including a job description, goals and a transition plan for your current role. Yes, this is a lot of work. However, if you enjoy working for that company and there aren't current positions that can lead to your version of success, you must do the hard work to create one. No one is as invested in your success as you are.

Set up time with your immediate boss to present the idea. Ask them for their thoughts. You'll want them to find problems with your proposal so that you have an answer or fix for potential issues before you have someone else – human resources or your supervisor's leader – look at it. Having your leader review the proposal first will give you an opportunity to gain their support and backing.

You may meet with some resistance, or even flat out refusal from your leader. If it's just resistance, ask questions to find out what the challenges are. Maybe they're concerned about the budget, or about how you will hand-off your responsibilities. Try to address the concerns by tweaking your proposal. You could even question them about how they would change it. Show your willingness to compromise. You need your supervisor to understand that you want to stay with this company, but you want to add value by addressing this unmet business need.

Refusal will be harder to deal with. If your boss is simply unwilling to consider a new position for you, you may need to work out the proposal with someone else. If your intent was to still report to your current supervisor, you'll need to re-work your idea. This is an instance where having a mentor or "board of advisors" will be extremely beneficial. Work with them to find a different path to the new position. If the new position was going to report to a different leader, request a meeting with that person and run the proposal past them. This may feel like you're going behind your manager's back after they told you no, but this is your career and they are already aware of your desire. You can, as a courtesy, let them know that you will also be presenting this to human resources or a different leader so they won't be surprised with any changes that may be coming.

Once the proposal is ready, you'll need to present your idea to whoever will be making the decision. Be prepared to show how this new role is the right thing for the company and why you are the person to do the job. You will need to sell the idea. Don't be afraid to talk about how you have the right skills and experience to take this on. Treat this as another job interview – but know that the stakes are higher because you are not only asking the decision maker to choose you, but also to choose to create the role you want.

The perfect scenario is that you go in well prepared. Your presentation is a hit – and the person you are presenting to loves your idea and approves it right away. Budget is in place and you can start in a few weeks as soon as you transition your current job to someone else. But, alas, we do not live in a perfect world. They may love your idea, but they can't make it work with the budget right now – especially if they need to hire someone to replace you in your current position. Or, maybe they see value in what you propose, but there are other priorities for the company, or for them. The good thing is, you've planted the seed and they love the idea. Now, you have to practice patience. Try to work out a timeline of when the move might be possible. Then, focus on your current work and finding other ways to be fulfilled in your job until the time is right.

The other possibility is that you'll be told no, and there isn't a possibility of creating this role, not now or in the future. You have to reflect, then, if you really want to stay with this company or seek out a similar position to the one you just created elsewhere. There is always opportunity, but you need to figure out what is more important to you.

Take the leadership position

Yes, the premise of this book is knowing that not everyone is cut out for leadership and we need to find different paths to success. Sometimes, though, the call to leadership is unavoidable. You are promoted into the position, for example, and there is no one else to do the job. You can still make it work.

Because you are not naturally inclined to leadership, you may need to delegate certain tasks. For example, if you struggle with making decisions, you might rely more on a participative leadership style. But you do need to be aware that style only works if you communicate very well. If you struggle with setting goals for your department – i.e., providing a strategy – meet regularly with your leader to determine your team's function in the organization's goals. Work with them to set goals and create a plan around how to reach those goals. Then, delegate tasks to your employees.

Often, someone moving from an individual contributor role to leadership struggles with not doing the work themselves. If this is the case, you can set parameters around what your work is and what your team's work is. Be sure there is someone in place that takes your old responsibilities. You may struggle with releasing control of those tasks. You can set up regular meetings with the employees who are now responsible for that work and also set up ways to measure the work so that you can be assured it is being done.

Partner with another leader that can help you with performing other management functions. This may be your current mentor, a peer, or another leader that you admire. Show a willingness and desire to learn and be coached.

You can also ask for feedback from the employees that report to you. There are a number of ways to do this. To set the stage, be open and honest in all communication with your team. This will build the relationship of trust. Be sure to ask how you can help them achieve their goals and ask other questions that lead to how you can support them better. As the relationship builds and you act on their feedback, the team will see that what they say matters. In time, you can ask questions that speak to your personal performance such as, "What can I do differently next time to better help you?"

You can also ask for feedback anonymously. Anonymous feedback is helpful if you feel like the team is fearful (whether justified or not) of commenting honestly. Explain how the process will work and how their input will remain anonymous and what you'll do with their feedback. Once the feedback is gathered, let the team know what you've learned and what changes may come of it.

Above all, do not get defensive. That's typically the hardest part of the process. You do want to learn and grow, so view the criticism as an opportunity and not a personal failure. You've already realized that leadership isn't your natural inclination, but you're here and you can make the best of the experience by turning it into a growth opportunity.

Chapter 12 - Still Want to Lead

Even after all the information you've gathered about yourself and how to find success outside of leadership, you may still want to go for a position leading people. Be aware, you'll probably need to work harder than someone that has an affinity for leading. You may also experience feeling more drained after a day of work than you might if you were in a role better suited to your strengths. As long as you're willing to put in the effort, you can make it work. There are a few things you can do to make your time as a leader less stressful and more productive.

Choose a role that uses your core strengths

You've already done the work to find what your strengths are, so use that information when you are looking for a leadership position that can best suit you. The first step (if you're not looking for a position in your current company) is to research different organizations. Find one that has a good cultural fit for you. If you want to be social at work and have outings with your colleagues outside of work, look for that type of environment before even looking for a position. Network with people at the company. If you don't already know someone there, find a connection who does and get introduced. Go back and read the information on building relationships in chapter 5 if you struggle with this. Networking is very important to finding the right fit in a job – current employees are the best resources to know how a company really operates.

After you find companies that have the right environment for you, then start looking for positions they have open. Use the job descriptions to match your areas of strength to their requirements for the position. You're in control here. You don't have to leave your current position and jump into the first leadership position that might be available. Take your time to make sure that you can use your knowledge, skills and abilities in the role.

Next comes the interview. Interviews are for both you and the company. You have another opportunity here to make sure that the position is something you can grow into and you will have the support you need. Challenge is good, but you don't want to set yourself up for failure in your first leadership position. Ask questions in the interview that provide you enough information to make an informed decision. Questions like, "How long has this team been in place?" or "What would signify a successful first 90 days for the person in this position?" These queries will give you insight into how much guidance you'll get from your direct leader, or even how much resistance a team might have to a new leader. You'll learn what you need to focus on in the beginning. If the answers to these questions make you uncomfortable or seem like something you don't want to take on, then don't! You don't need to move forward in the process. Take your time to find the best fit.

You can also ask questions related to your strengths or personality inclinations. If "competition" is one of your strengths, you can ask about how your performance would be rated. Or, if you are an ENTP Myers-Briggs personality type and you like to have open, honest debate and find holes in arguments, you would want to find out if questioning the status quo is encouraged. You would be miserable in an environment that didn't allow that sort of communication. Don't accept less for yourself.

Get educated

Each level of leadership requires a different skill set. Moving from an individual contributor to a first level leader will also involve knowing what work habits you will stop or change. This is an important point. So much emphasis is placed on learning new skills to become a leader, but you won't be successful if you can't stop working like you always did as an individual contributor.

When you're only responsible for yourself, generally, you focus on your career as it relates to you. Your mindset has to change as a leader. You are no longer the focus. You must now spend more time putting your employee's and your department's success first. This may sound counterintuitive to fostering your own success as a leader, but your success depends on how well you lead. So, in short, if they are successful, you are successful.

Some other differences in your work effort would include the reasons behind building relationships and how you get results. For example, as a new leader, your networking will be about meeting the right people for your team's benefit, not necessarily for your own personal development. You'll want to make sure you have the right connections to get your employees the tools and support they need and also the recognition they deserve.

As for results, previously, you would have done the job yourself – now you have to learn to get results through other people. Sometimes, managers do some of the work, but you can't perform in the same way you always did because you have too many responsibilities to other people now. You have to learn to delegate. If you don't know how to delegate (or maybe you're doing it incorrectly), take steps to develop that skill. That could mean taking a class on delegation, observing other leaders, reading good books on the subject, or working with your mentor.

Some companies offer new leadership training. Avail yourself of the opportunity. You should not go into the role with the mindset that you don't need any help. Too many new leaders let pride get in the way of acquiring knowledge. If you're going to step into this path, do it right. Take the time to learn the new skills you need to lead well.

Choose a mentor

Finding a mentor has been mentioned multiple times throughout this book. If I can point to one single thing that can help your success, in any capacity, it would be having a great mentor. I've already given you the steps to do this, but your strategy this time is to find a mentor that is a strong leader. This person is recognized by other leaders and employees alike as a role model in leadership. People want to work for and with this person. You admire this person's leadership ability – the way they lead and the outcome of their efforts. This person should also be a little bit like you. Meaning, they should have similar strengths as you do, maybe even similar weaknesses - someone who has been through similar experiences. Their guidance will be that much more valuable because they truly understand where you're coming from. That's who you want to mentor you.

Use feedback from your direct reports and your direct leader to gear the mentorship sessions. This isn't just about shoring up your shortcomings. While that's important, you will also spend a significant amount of time learning how to use your strengths in your leadership role. Remember, it's your responsibility to actively participate – listen, take the feedback and apply it to leading your team.

It can be helpful to look for specific situations in which you were unsure of your decision, actions or responsibilities. Write them down so you can review them with your mentor. You'll benefit more if you can come up with alternate ways of handling the circumstances and think of pros and cons to each solution. Your advisor can guide you through how to handle the situation the next time or explain how they might have handled similar circumstances. Most often, you'll find that your mentor is not going to give you the "answer." That's not teaching you the skills you need to think through the problem when they aren't available to help. The goal is to give you the tools you need to be the best leader you can – not to have you rely on others to get you through each situation.

Chapter 13 - Final Thoughts

I hope this book encouraged you to explore success from a different perspective. For some, it might have been enlightening to look at their careers differently. The trajectory isn't flat – even if you're not moving into leadership. You can explore different levels of individual contribution and teamwork. Ideally, you will have found that you can be passionate and completely fulfilled being in a role that uses your innate personality, strengths and talents, along with knowledge and skills you've picked up along the way.

Not everyone gets to be in a job they consider "play." But if you can go to a job that you feel good about doing because it speaks to your passions and you are energized at the end of the day, rather than drained – you are light-years ahead of others who consider work pure drudgery.

To find your personal success:

- Define what is important in your life and set goals around those areas
- Build relationships
- Be a servant
- Identify your preferences, strengths and skills, then apply them to your role
- Communicate – actively listen and give feedback
- Find a mentor, or two or three.

Take your time with the information in this book. As you think on all you've taken in, you might want to select one or two items to work on at a time and then move on. Read through chapters again when you're ready for the next challenge. Above all, remember that this is about you and finding your best fit. I wish you well on your personal journey of success.

Jennifer Raschig

Appendix

SMART Goals Worksheet

SPECIFIC: What exactly do I want to do?

MEASURABLE: How will I track my progress?

ATTAINABLE: Is this realistic? Who or what do I need to make it possible?

RELEVANT: Why does this matter to me?

TIMELY: When will this goal be completed?

Jennifer Raschig

Resources

Leader. (2015). Retrieved March 07, 2018, from https://www.merriam-webster.com/dictionary/leader
Shark Tank [Television series]. (n.d.). ABC.
State of the American Workplace (Rep.). (2017). Washington, D.C.: Gallup.
Achor, S. (2011). *The happiness advantage: The seven principles that fuel success and performance at work.* London: Virgin.
Brinkman, R. and Kirschner, R. (2002). *Dealing With People You Can't Stand.* New York: McGraw Hill.
Buckingham, M. (2005). *The One Thing You Need to Know …About Great Managing, Great Leading, and Sustained Individual Success.* New York: Free Press.
Cashman, K. (2003). *Awakening the Leader Within – A Story of Transformation.* Hoboken, NJ: John Wiley & Sons.
Charan, R., Drotter, S., and Noel, J. (2011). *The Leadership Pipeline – How to Build the Leadership Powered Company, 2nd Ed.* San Francisco: Jossey-Bass.
Citrin, J. M., & Smith, R. (2005). *The five patterns of extraordinary careers: The guide for achieving success and satisfaction.* New York: Three Rivers Press.
Ferrazzi, K. (2005). *Never Eat Alone and Other Secrets to Success, One Relationship at a Time.* New York: Double Day.
Fischer, R., & Sharp, A. (1998). *Getting It Done: How to Lead When You're Not In Charge.* New York: HarperCollins.
Gallup, Inc., (n.d.). Understand how your talents work with others. Retrieved April 1, 2019, from https://www.gallupstrengthscenter.com/home/en-us/cliftonstrengths-themes-domains.
Harrison, K. (2018, Jan 3). 4 Tips for Finding a Career Mentor. *Forbes.* Retrieved May 23, 2019, from https://www.forbes.com/sites/kateharrison/2018/01/03/4-tips-for-finding-a-career-mentor/#3d030b3752cf.

Hedges, K. (2015, March 31). New Rules! How Managers Can Be Friends With Employees. *Forbes*. Retrieved March 21, 2018, from https://www.forbes.com/sites/work-in-progress/2015/03/31/new-rules-how-managers-can-be-friends-with-employees/#53799e304c5b

Hoover, J. (2004). *How to Work For an Idiot: Survive and Thrive Without Killing Your Boss*. Franklin Lakes, ND: Career Press.

Kay, F. (2010). *Successful Networking: How to Build New Networks for Career and Company Progression*. Philadelphia: Kogan Page Limited.

Leider, R., & Shapiro, D. (2015). *Work Reimagined: Uncover Your Calling at Work*. Oakland, CA: Berrett-Koehler Publishers.

Loehr, J. & Schwartz, T. (2003). *The Power of Full Engagement*. New York: Free Press.

Matthews, G. (n.d.). Goals Research Summary. Retrieved February 4, 2019, from https://www.dominican.edu/academics/lae/undergraduate-programs/psych/faculty/assets-gail-matthews/researchsummary2.pdf.

Maxwell, John C. (1998). The 21 Irrefutable Laws of Leadership. Nashville, TN: Thomas Nelson, Inc.

McGrath, M. (2017, May 24). World's Largest Restaurant Companies, 2017: McDonald's Slips While Darden Makes Gains. Retrieved March 27, 2018, from https://www.forbes.com/sites/maggiemcgrath/2017/05/24/worlds-largest-restaurant-companies-2017-mcdonalds-slips-while-darden-makes-gains/#54c36e6c3822

Moses, B. (1998). *Career Intelligence: The 12 New Rules for Career and Life Success*. San Francisco: Berrett-Koehler Publishers.

National Center for O*NET Development. Personal Financial Advisors. *My Next Move*. Retrieved June 21, 2019, from https://www.mynextmove.org/profile/summary/13-2052.00

Patterson, K., Grenny, J., McMillan, R., & Switzler, A. (2012). *Crucial Conversations: Tools for Talking When the Stakes Are High*. 2nd Ed. New York: McGraw Hill.

Peter, L. J., & Hull, R. (2011). The Peter principle: why things always go wrong. New York: Harper Business.

Rath, T. (2015). *Are You Fully Charged?: The Three Keys to Energizing Your Work and Life.* Silicon Guild.

Rath, T. (2007). *StrengthsFinder 2.0.* New York: Gallup Press.

Sanborn, Mark. (2006). *You Don't Need a Title to Be a Leader.* New York: Double Day.

The Myers & Briggs Foundation. (2014). The 16 MBTI Types. Retrieved June 19, 2019, from https://www.myersbriggs.org/my-mbti-personality-type/mbti-basics/the-16-mbti-types.htm.

Tulgan, B. (2007). *It's OK to Be the Boss.* New York: HarperCollins.

Whitted, R. (2016). *Outgrow your space at work: How to thrive at work and build a successful career.* Grand Rapids, MI: Revell, a division of Baker Publishing Group.

###

Jennifer Raschig

About the Author

Thank you for reading my book! If you enjoyed it, please take a minute to leave me feedback at your favorite retailer.

Thank you!
Jennifer Raschig

Jennifer Raschig is an author, speaker, business consultant and professional organizer. With almost 20 years in leadership positions, she is experienced with creating order out of chaos for people and processes in the business world. Raschig realized that above all, her passion was in helping others relieve stress. Now, she is able to do this every day through her writing, speaking and coaching efforts. She has obtained degrees in Business Management and Accounting and is the author of <u>Living Within Your Means: A practical guide to financial freedom</u>. She lives with her husband and teenage boys in southeastern Wisconsin. To reach Jennifer, visit www.jenniferraschig.com.

www.ingramcontent.com/pod-product-compliance
Lightning Source LLC
Chambersburg PA
CBHW022105170526
45157CB00004B/1495